Abingdon Press

Contents

Fellowship Programs

MANUFACTURED IN THE UNITED STATES OF AMERICA

Cover Design: Kelly Chinn

03 04 05 06 07 08 09 10 11 12—10 9 8 7 6 5 4 3 2 1

Contents

Service Projects

Plan Now for Your Ministry Fair

Allocate a short amount of time at the beginning of the year to discuss the Ministry Fair idea. (See page 93.)

Gather and save materials (including photographs) from each activity. After each project, ask one or two tweens to write a short synopsis of the activity while it is fresh on their minds. Then your group will have something special to celebrate and to share at the Ministry Fair.

About the Writers

Mark Bushor is associate pastor of education and youth at St. Mark United Methodist Church, Cleburne, Texas. He is the author of *Mission Mania,* published by Abingdon Press.

Leigh L. Gregg is director of children and family ministries at Sierra Vista United Methodist Church, San Angelo, Texas. In addition, she serves as a local pastor assigned to Veribest United Methodist Church (a small rural congregation east of San Angelo). She has written for *Children's Teacher* and *Exploring Faith.*

James H. Ritchie, Jr., lives in Monroeville, Pennsylvania, where he writes curriculum, teaches, and serves as a consultant with Ritchie Faith Span Ministries. He developed the *Created by God* sexuality education resources, published by Abingdon Press.

James Wrede has served as youth director and children's pastor in several churches in northwest Texas; he now lives in Belleville, Illinois. He has written for *Exploring Faith* and for *Power Xpress.*

Celebrate Here While Moving Toward There

By James H. Ritchie, Jr., Ed.D.

Contrary to popular attitude, preteens have not contracted some incurable disease, although dis-ease is a prominent characteristic of young persons moving into adolescence. There is little that represents ease (restfulness, gentleness, or easiness) about the preteen years. While they can be tough years to negotiate, we do our tweens, ourselves, our churches, and our world a disservice when we effectively put young persons "on hold" or opt to simply endure them until such time as their hormones stabilize and they become us.

How do we move from tolerating to celebrating our preteens? We reach them, venturing beyond our comfort zones. We teach them, using methods that honor their developmental stage. We unleash them to serve in the name of Jesus Christ. We learn from them. Finally, we never turn from them—no matter how tempting that is at times.

Reach Them

Think in concrete terms. As the teachers, fellowship leaders, music directors, and worship leaders of preteens, start by remembering—a potentially painful but crucial experience. To reach out to preteens, one must first reach back and touch his or her own early adolescence. Recall your family situation when you were ten, eleven, or twelve years old. In particular, how did those dynamics seem to be altered by your emerging adolescence? Did parents or those serving as primary caregivers seem to be changing during those years—either becoming overly interested in your comings and goings, or taking a more "hands-off" approach as you matured? How did that feel? What about school? Any shift in academic performance? Think about those persons who were your closest friends? Did they change from earlier years? Did you find yourself becoming less tolerant of a particular group of persons? Consider how you believe that you were being perceived by other persons during those years. How did you categorize yourself then? What words might you use today to describe who you were then?

Now, how do you share those memories—be they painful, amusing, or poignant—with the tweens you relate to now? Take care to use language that helps to make connections between their experience and yours. If they sense this is "all about you," you will lose them. Daring to conjure up emotions associated with your own preteen years, as well as experiences, will give your words authenticity.

Teach Them

Persons who are committed to helping young persons make the transition from child to adolescent need to do a bit of tightrope walking. While preteens are becoming better equipped to handle abstract reasoning—applying truths or learnings from one situation to another, they remain concrete thinkers in many respects. Answers and perceptions still tend to fall on the opposite ends of the spectrum. Tweens need to be pushed gently to consider the ever-present grays in any given situation, and to anticipate the possible outcomes of their decisions or actions.

Too often we abandon learning activities that involve young persons physically—whether that be through artistic expression or movement. Finger paints are for kids! Older kids need to learn to sit still. Taking away hands-on, expressive media can leave them voiceless as they move into their preteen years. Yes, they need to learn how to engage in discussions, but oftentimes it is the "hands-on" experience that initiates the conversation.

Physical proximity makes a difference in working with preteens. While it is important to "give them their space," it is equally as important not to teach them at arm's length. As they lose touch with the child they once were but are no longer, they get to feeling

untouchable. Part of this is hormonal. Nothing feels the way it used to, nothing is right, so just back off. They are adjusting to their new selves. Part of it is relational. Staying close by gives wordless assurance that the world isn't abandoning them.

Unleash Them

The power of tweens needs to be unleashed on a world in need. While they are moving into years when the hormones rule all dimensions of life, they aren't there yet (in many cases). They have a great capacity for compassion that needs to be tapped. These are excellent years to connect them with adult mentors, and outreach experiences can be the best opportunities for this to happen.

Although family dynamics become more problematic with adolescence, these young persons continue to need meaningful, directional interaction with adults. When preteens have the chance to interact with groups of adults—including their parents, they begin to realize that their parents don't actually stick out like the sore thumbs they were fearing.

Preteens appreciate large projects. Coloring cards for nursing home residents just isn't going to go over. Their world is changing, so why shouldn't they change the world? Let them choose the projects, plan how to get the job done, and invite adults to help.

Learn From Them

Ask tweens what they think from time to time, and listen attentively to their responses. Put them on committees and make sure their voices are heard. Invite them in to interact with the members of an adult Sunday school class once in a while. Involve them in worship leadership on a regular basis, but don't abandon them as they prepare. Preteens want to do a good job. Rehearse with them in advance so they are comfortable in their leadership role—enough so that the worshipers will also be comfortable being led by a young person. Let them assist with preparing the liturgy. Guide them up front as to what is needed in order to avoid excessive editing. They need to be able to speak their own language and articulate their own thoughts. The congregation needs that.

Never Turn From Them

Tweens can be a handful at times, but what wonderful people to have your hands full of! Find ways to celebrate the wonders of the preteen years and to aid the transition from child to adolescent. Some churches have developed their own liturgical ways to do this—rites of passage. In some settings, confirmation can serve that role. Since young persons are going to be reluctant to have signs of the onset of puberty recognized in public (as has been done in other cultures and in other times), we need to focus on something such as their faith commitment at confirmation, or a transitional birthday such as 12 or 13. They could be assigned an adult and a youth mentor to walk them through the coming years and to accompany them on their faith journeys. This season may be a time to use the ritual for reaffirmation of the baptismal covenant. Choose a hymn that will become "their" hymn, and a Scripture passage to serve in the same capacity. Establish a specific project that could be funded by donations made in honor of young persons' transition into adolescence.

Reach them, teach them, unleash them, learn from them, and never turn from them. Preteens need the support of the community of faith as they move into and through the rigors of adolescence. Transitions are often feared, but when embraced with intentionality and compassion, the transition from child to adolescent can be more than tolerable or survivable—something worth celebrating.

Unexpected Prophets

Failing to listen to our tweens or to examine the world through their eyes, we run the risk of missing the prophetic word that God could be speaking to us through them. Does that make theirs the definitive perspective? No. But we decrease our chances of realizing the definitive perspective—that is, God's truth as determined by wisdom distilled from the group rather than from the individual—when we exclude the tweens' unique understanding of God, God's world, God's will, God's justice, and the role that Jesus Christ played and continues to play. Their ability to make significant contributions is not far off in the distant future, but is right now and right wherever you are. Unless we learn to celebrate our preteens in the here and now, we will not have the chance to celebrate them in the days ahead, because they will have managed to disappear from us.

Fellowship Programs

1 In a Foreign Land

LESSON IN A NUTSHELL

Many of the youth in your group will likely be new to your town or church or in a new school situation (moving from elementary to middle school or junior high, for instance). The lesson will help the tweens begin to adjust and to make new friends in their new environment.

IN A FOREIGN PLACE (5–10 MINUTES)

Take the group to a location that is not your usual meeting place. Have everyone look around the place.

Ask:

- How is this place different from where you are used to meeting?
- Does the difference make you uncomfortable?
- Why is it so difficult to adjust to new situations?

MAP OF MALAPROPRIA (10–15 MINUTES)

Divide the tweens into two or three groups. Give each group a copy of "Map of Malapropria" (page 9) and ask these questions. (None of the answers are available on the map.)

- How many yards to an inch? [There is no scale at all on the map.]
- What is this a map of?
- Where does the road on the east end of town lead?

After a few moments, bring everyone together and have them describe their experiences with this map.

Ask:

- If this were truly a map to a place you were visiting, could you get around?
- How would you figure out your way around town?

Before They Arrive

- ❑ Make two or three copies of "Map of Malapropria" (page 9).
- ❑ Arrange for the group to meet somewhere different from where you would usually meet. You can either meet at the different site or in your normal place and then head somewhere else as a group. Try to make the site a place with which the group is not familiar. Some suggestions include another church or a synagogue, the lobby of an office building, a warehouse, a barn (especially for non-farm tweens). Ideally, the group will feel out of their element in this place.
- ❑ Be sure to have consent forms signed by parents for traveling with the tweens if you are driving somewhere.

Supplies

- ❑ At least one Bible
- ❑ Song sheets, accompaniment
- ❑ Chairs (see Special Tips, on page 8)
- ❑ Copies of the map

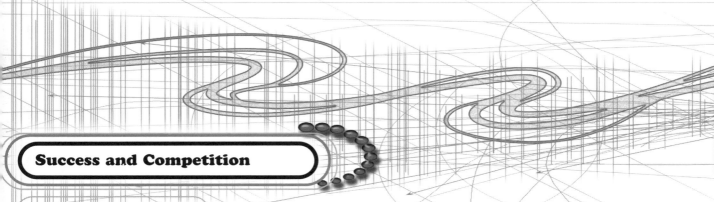

Special Tips

If the location for the meeting does not include chairs, improvise or use one of these games as an alternative:

Alphabetical I Have Never— Have participants form a circle, sitting on the floor or wherever available. The first person must say, "I have never" and name something beginning with the letter *A.* (I have never "*argued*" with my mother.") The next person must use a *B.* (I have never "*been*" to Mars.") Continue until everyone has had a chance.

OR

Yes or No—The tweens must quickly sort themselves into "yes" or "no." Designate one side of the room as "yes" the other as "no." Call out situations that have yes-or-no answers. Tweens must run to the correct side of the room. (Example: "I have eaten ice cream this week.")

I HAVE NEVER (15–20 minutes)

Have the group form a large circle with their chairs. One person stands in the middle (without a chair) and announces, "I have never____," saying some action they have not done. For instance, the first person might say, "I have never been fishing." Everyone in the group who has gone fishing must stand up and move to a different chair. The person in the middle attempts to sit in one of the vacated chairs. No one may return to the seat he or she just left during that same turn.

After several rounds of this, you may reverse the order to "I have ____." At this point, everyone who has not done the stated activity gets up and moves.

Close the game by asking everyone if they learned some interesting tidbits about others in the group (for example, "Gina has been to Norway"). Also, ask who of them might have felt odd at any point (such as when they were the only one who had not been fishing).

LOOK A LITTLE DEEPER (10–15 minutes)

Ask a volunteer to read aloud **Deuteronomy 10:12-22.**

Then ask:

- Who is being addressed in this passage?
- Why are the Hebrews told to "love the stranger" (verse 19)?

Say: **The Hebrews were establishing a new way of life. They had been slaves and told what to do by the Egyptians, but they were now free. God did not want them to forget who they were or where they had come from. God also wanted them to be aware of others who might also be in new situations.**

Ask:

- How do we handle new situations?
- How do we help others in new situations?

SENDING FORTH (5–10 MINUTES)

Gather the group and sing a few songs together. Ask the tweens to name any favorites they have. Tell them that these songs can help them remember who they are. Remind them that God is with them in new situations as well. Have them tell any prayer concerns they may have, especially for anything new in their lives. Pray.

Map of Malapropria

Directions

Look at the map at left. Then answer the following questions:

How many yards to an inch?

What is this a map of?

Where does the road on the east end of town lead?

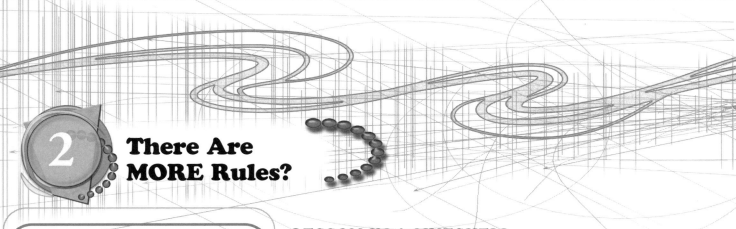

There Are MORE Rules?

Before They Arrive

- ❑ Make a copy of the handout "Old Testament Rules" (page 12) for each person.
- ❑ Write the Lord's Prayer on a large sheet of paper or markerboard for all to see; or make individual copies. Check your hymnal for the exact wording.

Supplies

- ❑ Bibles for all
- ❑ Paper and pencils or pens
- ❑ Copy of the Lord's Prayer

LESSON IN A NUTSHELL

Rules are an integral part of any group's functioning. This lesson is to help tweens understand why rules are necessary while at the same time making sense of the confusion the rules can create.

CONTINUOUS STORY (15–20 MINUTES)

Hand out sheets of paper. Tell the tweens to put their names at the top. Tell them to write a story, beginning with the words, "Every game has its rules, but. . . ." Once they have those words written down, they are to keep writing until you tell them to stop.

Once you stop them, tell them to fold over their papers so that only their last sentence is showing. Then they are to pass the paper to someone else. No one is to look at any part of the paper except for the last sentence. Have them continue the story where it leaves off, based on the one sentence each person sees. Tell the tweens to keep writing until you stop them.

Stop the tweens, have them fold and pass their papers again. Repeat the process at least two more times. Then have them open up the papers and return them to the original authors. Allow each author to read his or her story.

MAKING UP THE RULES (25–30 MINUTES)

Divide the group into three smaller groups. Tell each group to design a game for the entire group to play. They may do anything they want as long as (a) they remain in your meeting area, (b) the rules can be adhered to by everyone in the bigger group (for instance, they cannot set an age limit that keeps some from playing), and (c) the game is one that encourages teamwork and good sportsmanship. Encourage them to make use of supplies found in the room.

After you give the groups enough time to design their games, bring everyone together and play each group's game. Talk about the experience of making up the rules. How important is having rules?

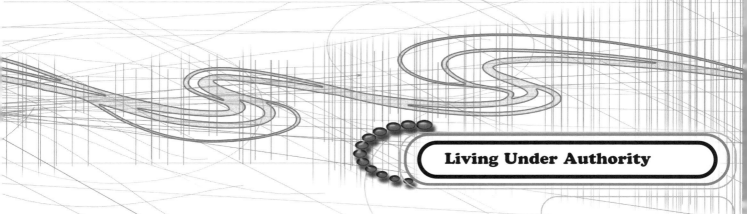

LOOK A LITTLE DEEPER (15–20 minutes)

Say: **Most people are familiar with the Ten Commandments. Did you know that the Old Testament actually has 616 commandments?**

Give everyone a copy of "Old Testament Rules" (page 12). Have the tweens follow the instructions on the page.

Direct the tweens to **Exodus 20 through 24.** Have them scan the laws there to find the answers. Also, have them read aloud any laws they find curious or interesting.

Ask:

- How easy would it be to follow all of these rules?
- Why were all of these rules necessary?
- How prepared would the Hebrew people have been without these rules?

Ask a volunteer to read aloud **Matthew 22:34-40.** Then ask:

- Jesus reduced everything to two rules. Are these enough?
- Why are rules necessary?
- Are there specific rules we should always follow?
- Are there some rules that do not need to be followed at all times?
- Do our rules ever change? Why?

SENDING FORTH (2–5 minutes)

Tell the group that you will be closing with the Lord's Prayer. While the odds are good that they are somewhat familiar with it, some tweens may not know it. It is quite likely that they will know a slightly different version. Direct them to the written version.

Say: **We are going to close our time together by praying the Lord's Prayer in a little different way today. At the end of each line, we are going to pause; and I want you to think about what that line means. I will cue us back in by saying, "Lord," before each next line.**

Pray the Lord's Prayer as a group.

When Time Matters

If you have less time:

"Making Up the Rules"—Instead of playing several games, start with a simple game such as Follow the Leader or Musical Chairs and invite one person at a time to add a new rule to the game.

If you have more time:

Add more games. Play board games before and/or after the lesson; or play other games such as Four Square, as your group sees fit.

Old Testament Rules Answers

1. Exodus 20:12

3. Exodus 20:4

4. Exodus 23:17

5. Exodus 23:1

6. Exodus:21-28

7. Exodus 23:10—
   Seventh year let it rest.

10. Exodus 23:4

Others are not in the Bible.

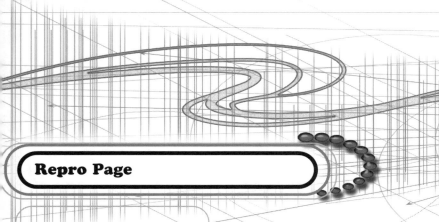

Old Testament Rules

Directions

To the right are several rules from the Old Testament (and a few added just for fun).

Decide which of them actually occur in the Old Testament (in Exodus 20–24) and cross out the ones that do not.

1. Honor your mother and father.

2. Cleanliness is next to godliness.

3. Do not make for yourself an idol or graven image.

4. Three times in the year all of your males shall appear before the Lord God.

5. You shall not spread a false report.

6. When an ox gores a man or woman to death, the ox shall be stoned.

7. You shall work your land every year, without fail.

8. You shall listen to your local Christian rock station, for the other music pleases me not.

9. Keep the room of your older sibling clean.

10. When you come upon your enemy's ox or donkey going astray, you shall bring it back.

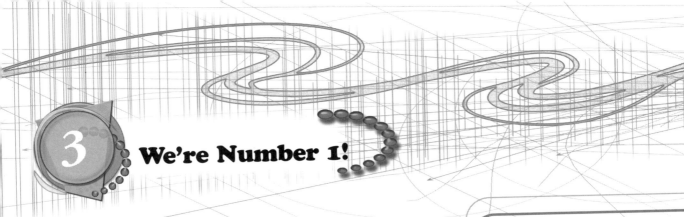

3 We're Number 1!

LESSON IN A NUTSHELL

We are a culture obsessed with winning. This lesson will look at our desire to be the best and how we are to behave as Christians.

THE GREATEST (10–15 minutes)

Hand out paper and pens or pencils. Challenge the tweens to write down as many words as they can, using only the letters found in the word *greatest.* Each word must have three or more letters, must be a common noun (no names of people or places), and must appear in an English dictionary. Also, each person may use only one form of each word (do not merely add *-s* or *-es*).

Give the tweens four or five minutes to work in silence.

Ask everyone to tell one or two words from his or her word list. Write on a large sheet of paper or markerboard each word someone has found. Let everyone have a chance to contribute before gathering more words from people who have several words. Add a few yourself if you see some that the group did not report finding. Celebrate the large list of words you found as a group.

HUMAN PYRAMIDS (10–15 minutes)

If you have ten or more people, divide the group into two or more groups. (Try to keep at least five in each group.) Otherwise, keep them all together. Tell each group that they have a challenge—to build the best pyramid that they can, using only themselves. Have the groups make their attempts at the same time, using gym mats as a cushion for the floor. (Be sure to have adults nearby to ensure safety in the group's efforts.)

Most people will assume that the height of the pyramid is the main objective; but choose some other, less obvious criterion, such as sturdiness, symmetry, or even the facial expressions of everyone involved. If the tweens catch on early, compliment them; but remain vague about the judging criterion. Compliment or critique the groups based on whatever criterion you use. (Note: Do not be negative in any critiques—just point out how the pyramid didn't meet the criterion that you were looking for.)

Before They Arrive

- ❏ On a markerboard or large sheet of paper, write the word *greatest.*
- ❏ Write the words to the "Prayer of Saint Francis" (page 15) on a markerboard or large sheet of paper.
- ❏ Be sure to have adults and gym mats on hand for Human Pyramids.

Supplies

- ❏ Bibles for all
- ❏ Paper and pencils or pens
- ❏ Markerboard or large sheet of paper and markers
- ❏ Gym mats

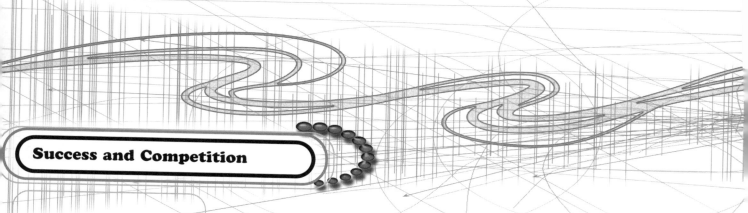

Gather everyone together and let them comment on the experience, recounting their successes, grousing about your criterion, and so on. Then ask:

- What makes someone successful?

TIC-TAC-TOE-A-THON (5–10 minutes)

Divide the group into pairs and provide each pair with a pencil and a sheet of paper. Tell them they are to play five games of tic-tac-toe against the person they are facing and must win three to advance to the next round. They are to replay any ties.

Pair any advancing players and have them play for the best of seven games. If players keep advancing, let them play until they cannot (coming in yourself and playing for the tie, if necessary). However, it should become obvious that two players who know the game cannot lose to one another; and therefore, no one can win. If anyone points this out at the beginning, have everyone play at least five games to witness this in action.

Ask:

- If two people are competing against each other, is there always a winner and a loser?

LOOK A LITTLE DEEPER (10–15 minutes)

Ask a volunteer to read aloud **Mark 10:35-45.** Ask:

- What did James and John want?
- How did Jesus respond?
- Did James and John get the answer they expected?

Say: **But we have been given other images of competition in the Bible.**

Read aloud **1 Corinthians 9:24-27,** then ask:

- Is Paul saying that only one of us will win God's blessings?
- How does this compare with what Jesus told James and John?

Say: **Our culture is a competitive one. Most people believe that there can be only one winner and a whole bunch of losers.**

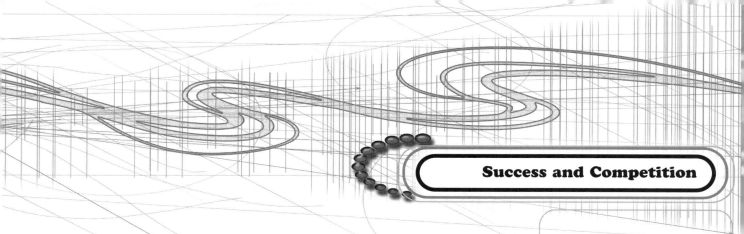

Ask:

- How does the Christian message compare with this?
- Are there exceptions to our culture's "win at all costs" mentality?
- What can you do to strive for excellence, as Paul suggests, yet still be within Christ's vision of greatness?
- Is it possible to succeed in our culture and still be a Christian?

SENDING FORTH (2–5 minutes)

Direct the tweens' attention to the words of "The Prayer of Saint Francis." Explain that St. Francis was a man who embraced the simple life and taught that simplicity leads one closer to God. In this saint's eyes, we are all winners when we choose to follow Jesus' way of life. Pray the prayer as a group.

The Prayer of Saint Francis

Lord, make me an instrument of thy peace;
where there is hatred, let me sow love;
where there is injury, pardon;
where there is doubt, faith;
where there is despair, hope;
where there is darkness, light;
and where there is sadness, joy.

O Divine Master,
grant that I may not so much seek
to be consoled as to console;
to be understood, as to understand;
to be loved, as to love;
for it is in giving that we receive,
it is in pardoning that we are pardoned,
and it is in dying that we are born to eternal life.

—Francis of Assisi, Italy, 13th Century

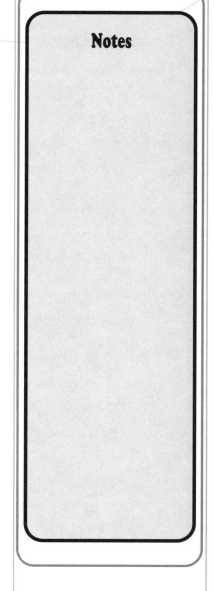

Notes

4 Stand Up? I AM Standing Up!

LESSON IN A NUTSHELL

Courage is a word that evokes mystery. How does someone have courage? The lesson will help tweens to explore this question.

STANDING TOGETHER (5–8 minutes)

Have all of the tweens form a circle, holding hands and then numbering off. Those who have an even number lean forward, and those with an odd number lean back (every other person). Then they do the opposite of what they did (the evens lean back and the odds lean forward). They have to lean as far as they can while maintaining a standing position.

Nobody will be able to pull the circle down. The point is to depend upon one another (our "friends in faith") to remain standing while leaning backward and forward. Standing together is one way to have courage.

TAKE A STAND (5–15 minutes)

Present your group with one of these topics:

- Christians should not have close non-Christian friends.
- Christians should not listen to non-Christian radio.

Tell the group that each person must decide whether he or she agrees or disagrees with the statement. Give the tweens a few minutes to think of their reasons. Then have each one give a brief summary of why he or she agrees or disagrees.

This activity can develop into a debate, but do not spend too long with the actual debate itself. The objective is to get each person to take a stand and defend it. Once everyone has presented and defended a point of view, end the debate.

Say: **Some subjects can be debated for a long time. That is not what this is about, however. What this activity had us do is take a stand on an issue and present it, even if others disagreed with us or presented an argument for which we had no answer. This activity is about showing courage.**

Before They Arrive

- ☐ Read Daniel 6 and prepare to tell the story.
- ☐ Make enough copies of "Proclaim Your Courage" for each person, including adults.
- ☐ For the Take a Stand activity, ask an adult volunteer to be ready to take a stand contrary to the prevailing stance if the tweens tend to line up on one side. This adult needs to make sure he or she challenges the other views as a participant and not as an authority figure, Be clear with the tweens so they do not take what the adult says as the definitive word on the subject.
- ☐ Set up the playing area for the game.

Supplies

- ☐ Bibles for all
- ☐ 2–5 utility balls (rubber balls about the size of a basketball)

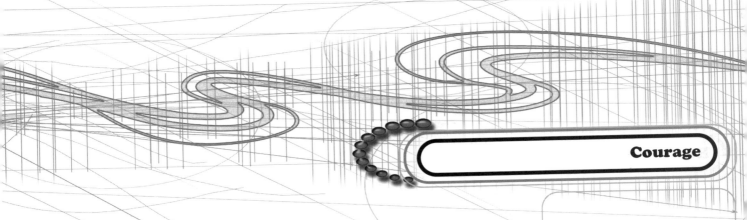

Say: *Courage* means, literally, "to take heart." It means doing something that is so important to you that you must do it, or you will feel defeated. It is standing up for your beliefs. Sometimes, we know it takes our hearts, because we feel them pumping and thumping far more than usual. We show courage when we act as we know is right for us, despite wishing that we did not have to.

LOOK A LITTLE DEEPER (10 minutes)

Set up the story of Daniel in the lions' den. Then have the tweens read **Daniel 6:10-18.** Many in the group may already know this story, but have them pay attention to the details—especially how Darius and Daniel respond.

Ask:

- Why did Daniel's peers plot against him?
- What was Daniel's response to the king's interdict?
- What was King Darius's response to Daniel's predicament?
- Which actions in this story were acts of courage?

PROCLAIM YOUR COURAGE (5–20 minutes)

Say: **While it is doubtful that any of us will face being thrown to the lions, Daniel's challenge is no different than many of our own. The "den of lions" is often the ridicule of our classmates and others, for example.**

Ask:

- What other "dens of lions" do we face?

Have the tweens choose one or more of the lions'-den situations. Have volunteers form teams to roleplay how they might take a stand to make things better. Affirm their efforts.

SENDING FORTH (2–5 minutes)

Hand out the "Proclaim Your Courage" worksheets. Go over the instructions. After the group has finished, challenge everyone to read his or her declaration. Applaud everyone for, at least, considering the worksheet, noting that courage is greatest where fear is greatest.

End the prayer with thanksgiving to the presence of God's Holy Spirit in our lives, which gives us courage.

When Time Matters

If you have more time:

"Proclaim Your Courage"—Do more roleplays or have more than one team present their way of addressing the situation so that tweens see some alternative ways of addressing problems that require courage.

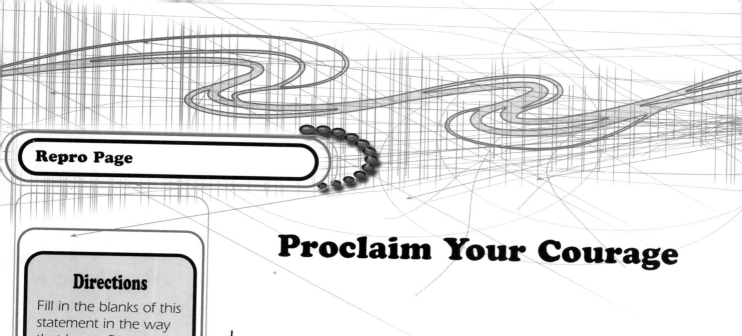

Proclaim Your Courage

Directions

Fill in the blanks of this statement in the way that best reflects how you feel.

I, _____, do hereby courageously proclaim Jesus Christ as my Lord and Savior. In addition, I freely declare that I am afraid of _____

_____,
but I trust that God will give me the strength to face that fear and overcome it. I also admit that I worry too much about

_____,
but I know that God is at my side.

I freely declare that I am wholly dependent upon the grace of God and the guidance of the Holy Spirit to get me through each day. Thank you, God, for your love of me! Amen!

Signed _____

Date _____

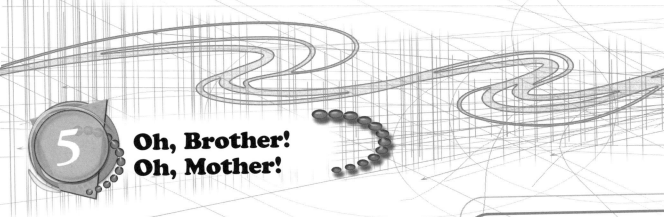

5. Oh, Brother! Oh, Mother!

LESSON IN A NUTSHELL

This lesson examines the role of the family and challenges everyone to take a look at the relationships in his or her own family.

ABSTRACT OF A FAMILY (10–20 minutes)

Ask the tweens to paint or draw a picture of their family, using one or more of these guidelines:

- Focus on what you value about your family. It may be togetherness, travel, a place to stay, and so on—as long as you value it and your family is a part of it.
- Include anything unique about your family (for instance, your family may celebrate its heritage, or everyone might play an instrument).
- Use colors to reflect your family. Maybe everyone wears green a lot. Perhaps your family is happy, and sunshiny yellow would fit them. Use your imagination.
- If you are having a hard time, think of one specific moment in your past that was really positive. Perhaps your family recently went on a great camping trip. Use the campsite to represent your family.
- Be as detailed or as vague as you want, but have something in the picture so that you could recognize what you were saying about your family if you came across it a year from now. It may be a family reunion or simply a big fish—as long as you can explain its significance, it is OK.
- Your picture may include your family members, but this is not a portrait. Accuracy and skill are not as important as creating an impression.

This activity may be challenging for some. Encourage them to think beyond the usual "mother, father, two sisters, and a cat" in their art, but do not force them. Have the tweens show and tell about their artwork.

FAMILY TO-DO LIST (10–15 minutes)

Tell the group to write at least ten things they can do with their family during the next month—anything from having fun to getting

work done—as long as they are ideas for things they can do together. Encourage the tweens to be realistic yet also creative in their ideas.

Have everyone tell some of his or her ideas. Then challenge the group to convince their families to adopt one or more of their ideas. You may wish to talk about any barriers the tweens see to following through with their ideas. Have the group come up with good approaches or alternatives for getting the family involved.

PICKING FAVORITES (10–15 minutes)

Give everyone a copy of "Picking Favorites." Go over the instructions.

After the tweens have had time to finish the worksheet, allow them to talk about some of their answers for the listed categories. Tell them that they may not talk about answers for the Bonus Question yet.

Ask the tweens whether they had any difficulty deciding their favorite for each category. Then ask:

- What did you think of the Bonus Question? Did it shock you?
- Was it tough to answer?
- Did any of you choose not to answer it? If so, why not?
- Was it too easy for some of you to answer? (*Move quickly to the next statement.*)

Say: **In some families, it is easy to see that some people have favorites. This can lead to very awkward situations. We are going to look now at one such family in the Bible.**

LOOK A LITTLE DEEPER (15–20 minutes)

Read aloud **Genesis 25:19-34; 27,** then ask:

- What kind of relationship did Jacob and Esau have from the beginning?
- How did Jacob trick both his father and his brother?
- What was Esau's response?

Say: **Families can be a source of great joy and support. They can also be a great deal of trouble. Most families are a mix of both.**

Ask:

- Why are families necessary?
- Are they sometimes difficult to deal with? How?
- Why can't we all have "perfect" families?
- What kinds of things can we do to make our family better for everyone in it?

SENDING FORTH (2–5 minutes)

Say: **Not all families are perfect, but everyone needs a sense of "family." As Christians, we are all part of God's family. That means that God loves us as God's own sons and daughters and that we are to love and support our "brothers and sisters" in Christ.**

Direct the tweens (and their families, if they join the group for the closing) to pray for one another this week. Have each tween talk with another tween (and each adult talk with another adult) to share with someone else a situation or a family member they would like that person to pray for during this week.

Say: **This request may mean praying for parents, stepparents, guardians, siblings, cousins, aunts, uncles, and grandparents. It may mean praying for healing between family members. It really means looking after one another the way brothers and sisters ought to, whether related siblings do it or not.**

Allow everyone a few moments to share together. Then close in prayer as a group. Lift up everyone's family during this time.

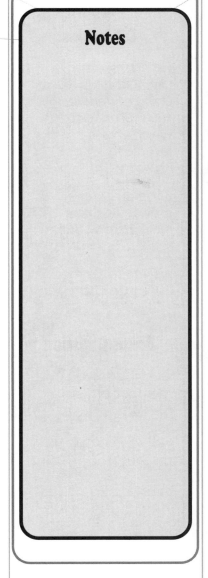

Notes

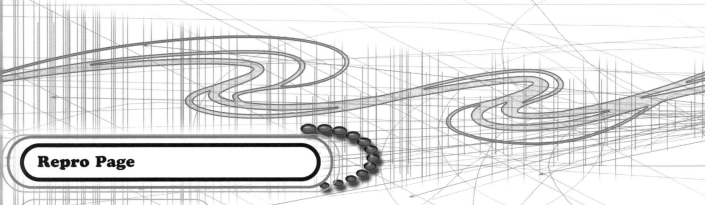

Picking Favorites

Directions

Each of these categories has several choices listed after it. You must decide which choice is your favorite for that category.

Circle one of the provided choices or write your own in the space provided.

Be sure to do the Bonus Question last!

Bonus Question

Pick your favorite member of your family:

Father, mother, sister, brother,

_____

Food: Pizza, Baked Potato, Hamburger, Chicken, _____

Style of Music: Pop, Country, Hip Hop, Jazz, _____

Color: Red, Blue, Purple, Green, _____

Type of Movie: Action, Romance, Comedy, Science Fiction,
_____

Day of the Week: Monday, Wednesday, Friday, Sunday, _____

Hairstyle: Beehive, Mohawk, Dreadlocks, Bald, _____

Non-English Language: Spanish, Japanese, Swahili, Esperanto,
_____

Dance Move: Bunny Hop, Electric Slide, Mashed Potato, Funky Chicken,
_____

Subject: English, Math, Social Studies, Science, _____

Number: 1, 7, 10, 322, _____

Direction: North, South, Southwest, North Northeast, _____

Animal: Dog, Tiger, Llama, Chicken, _____

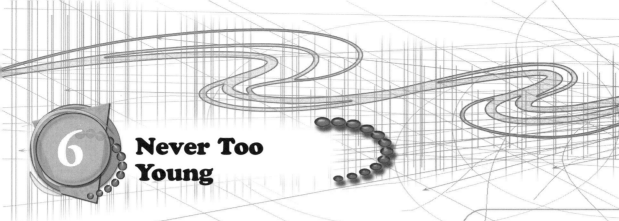

6 Never Too Young

LESSON IN A NUTSHELL

This lesson lets the tweens know that they can make a difference in life right now.

WHAT'S THE MINIMUM AGE? (5–10 minutes)

Have the group do "What's the Minimum Age?" (page 26).

If you cannot find appropriate materials for your group to use during the meeting time, have the tweens make guesses; ask them to explain why they guessed the age they did. Give the correct answers. You may need to research the answers that vary by state.

Answers: 1. depends upon the church denomination; 2. 18; 3. varies by state (usually age 15 with a licensed driver, 16 unaccompanied); 4. 25; 5., 7., 8. and 9. varies by state; 6. no minimum age; 10. varies by bank (usually no minimum age)

WHO WAS THE YOUNGEST? (10–15 minutes)

Ask everyone to turn over the handout, number from 1–7, and write his or her answer to each of the following questions:

1. How old were you when you first saw a movie at a theater?
2. How old were you when you first traveled out of your home state?
3. How old were you when you first rode a bicycle without training wheels?
4. How old were you when you entered your first competition?
5. How old were you when you first played miniature golf?
6. How old were you when you first sang a solo? or performed in some other way, such as dance or play an instrument?
7. How old were you when you first spent the night at a friend's house?

After everyone has answered these questions, have the class guess who in the group was the youngest to do each of the listed activities. After compiling guesses for each answer, ask everyone to give his or her answer.

Before They Arrive

❑ If it is possible, plan to have your meeting someplace the group can do research, such as a library or in a home or office with an Internet connection. You might also bring supplies such as your state's drivers' manual; a source book on American government (or even the Constitution); or printouts of various data, including state marriage laws.

❑ Arrange for your group to be with younger children—whether the children join your group or you go to them. Preschoolers in a program meeting at the same time would be ideal. Be sure to check with the leaders of the children's group in advance. See "Embracing Children" (on page 24) for details. This activity is for your group's benefit as much as (if not more than) the younger group's.

❑ Make enough copies of "What's the Minimum Age?" (page 26) for each person.

Supplies

❑ See the list above.
❑ Bibles for all
❑ Pencils or pens

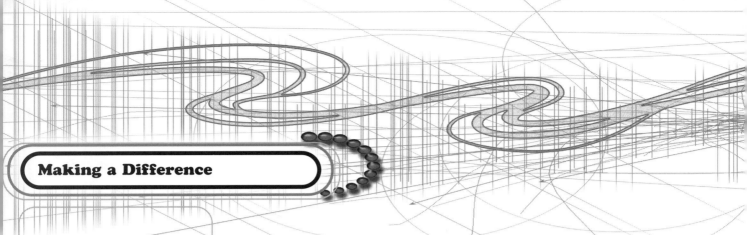

Making a Difference

When Time Matters

If you have less time:

"What's the Minimum Age?"—Do this activity as the tweens arrive or go straight to the next activity. Try to preserve as much time as possible for the activity with the children and the Bible study.

If you have more time:

"Look a Little Deeper"— Assign one or more of the three stories to volunteers to act them out.

EMBRACING CHILDREN (15–30 minutes)

Tell the group that they are going to play some games with younger children. Ask the tweens to pay particular attention to how the younger kids look to them. Remind them that they are much older than the little ones. Their job is to have fun, but to do so at the younger kids' level.

Play games such as Duck, Duck, Goose or Tag as a group and then break into smaller groups (or one-on-one) to just play with toys, color, and so on.

After some time playing together, bring your group back together and bid the younger group farewell. Then ask:

- How did the young children treat you?
- How did you feel as you played with them?

LOOK A LITTLE DEEPER (10–15 minutes)

1 Samuel 16–17 includes three important stories:

- God choosing the unlikely youngest son to be king;
- Young David soothing the mentally ill king with his music; and
- Young David facing the giant Goliath on the battle field.

Read these stories in advance and tell them in an interactive way to the tweens, inviting them to supply details of the plot as they know it. Be dramatic—have fun with the retelling. Ask:

- Was David an adult when God chose him to be the king of Israel?
- Why did God choose him?
- How did David respond to God's call?
- How did David use his gifts, even though he was young?
- How did the Israelites respond to David at first? How did Goliath respond?

Have everyone read together **1 Timothy 4:12.** Ask:

- What does this verse mean?
- What is too young? too old?
- Does the "right" age depend on the circumstances?
- What can you do right now?
- What can you do as part of the church?

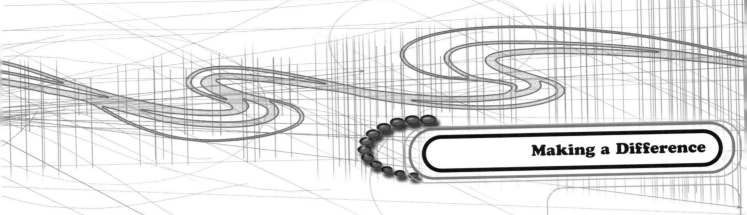

Talk about ways the tweens can make a difference both within the church and through the church. Encourage them to use the power they have as part of the body of Christ to make positive changes in the lives of others.

SENDING FORTH (2–5 minutes)

Say: **God has called you to be an active part of the church. Let's pray together and thank God for the many ways in which we are blessed. Remember, your life is not ahead of you; your life is right now!**

Take prayer requests for the week. Pray as a group.

Notes

You may want to talk with your pastor about specific opportunities that are available to tweens. Can they serve on church committees? be part of a congregational service or mission project? take leadership in worship?

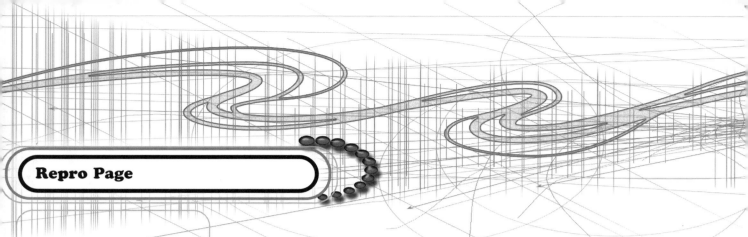

What's the Minimum Age?

Directions

Using the materials available, find out what the minimum ages are for these significant events in your state.

If no materials are available, then make your best guess. Be prepared to tell why you think your choice is the right one.

1. Take Communion

2. Vote for public officials

3. Drive a car

4. Run for United States House of Representatives

5. Drive a motorcycle

6. Speak up to adults for your beliefs

7. Marry

8. Fly alone in an airplane

9. Start a business

10. Open a bank account

7 I Can't Take It Anymore!

LESSON IN A NUTSHELL

This lesson examines stress and helps tweens both identify it and find ways to overcome it.

STRESS-O-METER (5–10 minutes)

Give everyone a copy of "Stress-O-Meter" (page 30). Go over the instructions with them.

After a few moments, go over the worksheet with the group. Then ask:

- Did you find this activity stressful?
- Did anything surprise you? If so, what?

Say: **This simple exercise cannot really tell you how stressed you may or may not be. What it does do is help you think about the stress in your life.**

PRESSURE COOKER (5–15 minutes)

Gather the group into a circle. Hold up a cup and show it to the group. Tell everyone that you are going to pass the cup around and that everyone has to say what the object is (a cup). Allow everyone to do that. When the cup returns to you, pull out another object (from your "bunch of miscellaneous objects") and pass the new object around. Tell everyone that, this time, he or she is to name not only the new object, but also any object that has already passed by.

After this object finishes the circle, and you are sure that the tweens understand the rules, introduce another object. Once you have passed it on, continue to add more and more objects. It will not be very long before a logjam starts to form, as players try to remember what objects have already passed when they are naming each one.

You do not need to recite each item that has already passed; just keep introducing new ones and encouraging the group to keep up with the game.

After the game has degenerated beyond all recognition (or you feel that enough is enough), gather the items back up and ask:

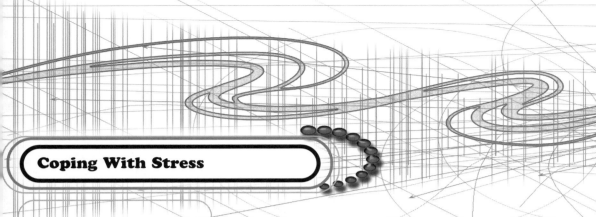

When Time Matters

If you have less time:

"Mini Golf"—Set up nine holes before the group arrives and play only those holes.

Think About It

Golf, a lovely little game designed to relieve stress, is often the source of more stress.

- Was it stressful to keep up with every object?"

If your group is handling this game rather easily, increase the speed of your hand-offs and keep objects already named in play. If they still do not have enough chaos, start naming objects inaccurately (for example, holding a ruler and calling it a bison).

MINI-GOLF (35–45 minutes)

Divide the tweens into groups of two to five people. Ideally, you will have three, six, or nine groups and at least one putter for each group. Each group is charged with designing two or three holes in a mini-golf course running throughout your meeting facility (if six or nine groups, 18 total holes; (three groups, 9 total holes).

Assign each group its available area. You may provide the tweens with supplies to create the obstacles or they may use whatever they find. Each hole needs a cup as its target.

Once the course is assembled, gather the group and walk the course together. Have each small group explain the path and challenges of their holes. After the walk-through, each group is sent through the course with a scorecard and at least one putter and one ball. You decide whether to play for individual scores or have each group record the best individual score for each hole as the team score.

LOOK A LITTLE DEEPER (10–15 minutes)

Ask a volunteer to read aloud **Luke 12:22-31.** Ask:

- What does Jesus say about worry?

Ask for volunteers to dramatize **Mark 4:35-41** (Jesus calms the storm). After their presentation, ask:

- How does faith help you deal with the stresses and worries in your life?
- What are ways you put yourself "in the boat with Jesus"? (*by following him, through prayer, and through trusting in God*)
- What are other positive ways we can handle stress? (Make a list of their responses for all to see. Some possible responses: *Talk with a friend; pray; write about the event and your feelings in a journal or letter to God; do something nice for someone else; play, run, do something physical; set priorities; be more selective about how many projects you take on.*)

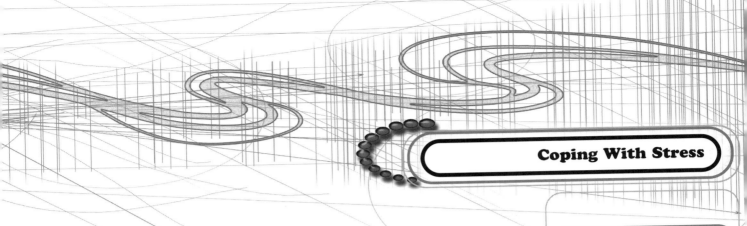

SENDING FORTH (6–8 minutes)

Sometimes, when the stress gets to be too much, we need to spend time alone with God. To close this meeting, give everyone the opportunity to do just that. Let them know that you will be giving them five minutes, which may seem like a long time because most of us are not used to spending quiet time. Assure them that you will call them back together at the end of the time so that they may relax and simply be with God.

They may wish to reflect on how God might be speaking to them and what God might be asking them to do with themselves now. Or they may simply rest in the assurance that God is handling the stressors in our lives.

With this instruction, send them throughout the meeting space to sit quietly with God. Do not let them talk to one another or leave adult supervision until this silent time is finished.

At the end of five minutes, call the group together (perhaps with music). Pray with thanksgiving for God's presence and love and for giving us peace in the midst of the storms in our lives.

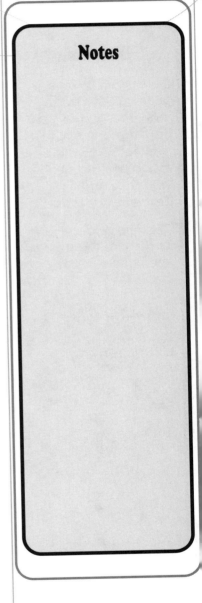

Notes

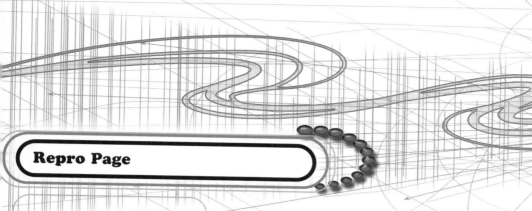

Stress-O-Meter

Directions

Rank the following areas of your life by how much stress you feel from them. Use a scale of 1–5, with 1 being "not stressed" and 5 being "extremely stressed."

Then add up the total and check the scale at the bottom of the page.

_____ School, homework

_____ Parents, siblings

_____ Friends, social

_____ Schedule, activities

_____ Rivals, bullies

_____ Money

_____ Possessions, games, stuff

_____ **Total**

Add up the total number and find yourself below:

7–14	15–21	22–28	29–35
Calm & Peaceful	Generally OK	Somewhat Stressed	HELP! HELP! HELP!

8 What a Character!

LESSON IN A NUTSHELL

This lesson examines the issues of character and integrity. Each individual will learn what these words are really all about and a Christian approach to integrity.

CONFUSED SCRIPT (10–15 minutes)

Provide everyone with a copy of "Confused Script" (page 34), and read the directions together. Then read the script as written. Let the group decide how they would alter the script. The easiest way to approach this task is look at the script, line by line, and ask the group what changes, if any, need to be made for this line to work. Remind them to keep an eye on how the final script will look after they have made the adjustments.

This activity may be challenging for some groups. It is a good idea for you to look at it ahead of time and see how you would change the script. Don't worry about how your modifications turn out; this exercise is to help get the group looking at the role of consistency and integrity.

After you have read the modified script, ask:

- Why were the changes necessary?
- Did they help the skit make more sense?

WHAT A CHARACTER! (10 minutes)

Invite everyone to draw on the back of the handout his or her favorite TV or movie character or something to symbolize that character.

Have several members of the group name their favorite characters. Write their answers on a markerboard or large sheet of paper. Ask:

- What do you like about these characters?
- Are any of them role models? (That is, should their actions and attitudes be mimicked?)
- Why are some characters generally well liked and others generally disliked?
- What is the difference between a hero and a villain?

Before They Arrive

❏ Make enough copies of "Confused Script" (page 34) for each person. Look at the script to decide how you would change it.

Supplies

❏ Bibles for all
❏ Markers, pens, or pencils
❏ Markerboard or large sheet of paper and markers

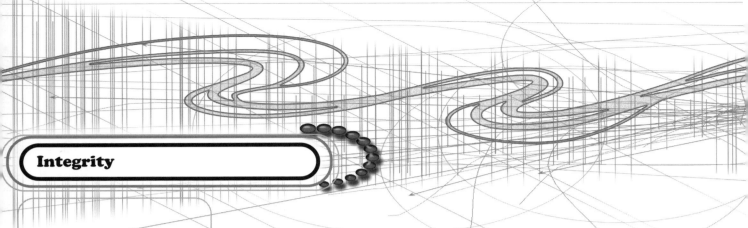

When Time Matters

If you have less time:

"Confused Script"— Instead of rewriting the script (from the reproducible), have the group talk about why the script does not make sense as written. Then jump to the last paragraph of the activity.

DESERT ISLAND (15–20 minutes)

Divide the group into smaller groups. Tell the groups they are survivors of a plane crash that has left them on a desert island. Challenge them to decide what five tasks they need to accomplish first. Then tell them they will be there indefinitely. Ask them to decide what qualities they want everyone on the island to show, starting with the leader and working through everyone else.

LOOK A LITTLE DEEPER (10–15 minutes)

Read aloud **1 Timothy 6:11-12, 17-19.** Have the tweens pay extra attention to verse 11. Ask:

▪ About what good character traits does Paul tell Timothy?

Say: **Many people talk about the concepts of "character" and "integrity," especially politicians (usually when attacking their opponents) and teachers (who want you to learn these traits).**

Ask:

▪ What are they talking about with these terms? What do they mean?

Allow a few moments for the tweens to answer this question. Invite them to give some examples.

Then say: **_Character_ is a word we are familiar with, since we use it in storytelling. The characters are the people we are following in whatever book we are reading or show we are watching. Their actions tell us a lot about who they really are. Usually, we cheer for the characters whose actions are closest to the values we hold, while we boo those who act against our values. When we speak of the character of an individual, it is the same—we are assessing whether we feel that he or she deserves a cheer or boo.**

Integrity means being complete and undivided. We talk of a building's integrity when we know that it is as solid as it was designed to be and will not collapse on us. Integrity is similar with people—we know where people with integrity stand and know that they will not collapse on us. We know that they mean what they say and will do their best to act in the way they say they will act.

Ask:

- Does this mean that people who agree with us are people of good character and integrity?
- Do you consider yourself a person of good character and integrity?
- What would you change to have a more complete and undivided life?

SENDING FORTH (3–6 minutes)

Say: **Integrity is a personal thing. While other people can often tell whether you have it, it is up to you to decide whether to have it. Spend a several moments alone and ask yourself this question:**

- What do I need to change in my actions or my thoughts to lead a life more pleasing to God and more appropriate for me?

Allow everyone to find a space where he or she can sit alone and reflect upon this question. After a while, call the group back together and have a closing prayer.

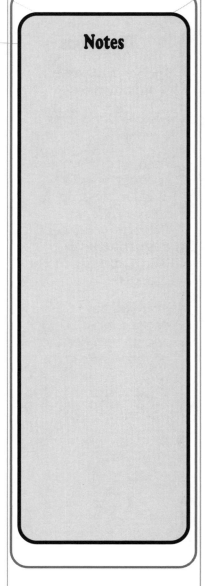

Notes

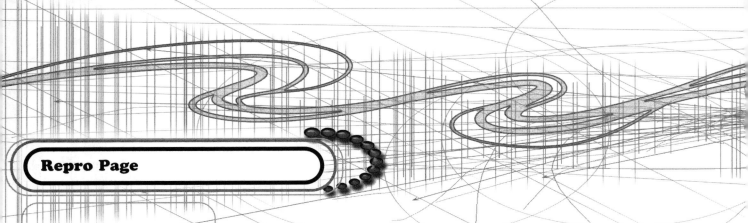

Confused Script

Directions

This script makes no sense as written.

First, read the script as a group.

Then, decide what changes need to be made to the script for it to make sense. Characters may need to switch lines or words may need to be changed.

After you have decided what adjustments need to be made, reread the script.

Coach: OK class! Let's divide into teams. Boys on my left and girls on my right.

Susan: You're not on our side, Thomas!

Coach: Oh? My mistake!

Coach: Thomas, get over with the girls this instant!

Thomas: Yes, Coach!

Coach: OK. I want you to line up from shortest to tallest. Then I'll divide you into teams.

Susan: Richard, stop pushing me.

Coach: What's the matter, Thomas?

Thomas: Nothing, Coach. We're all right.

Coach: Coach? Should we leave a space for Rhonda?

Coach: No. These teams are just for today's games.

Thomas: Uh, Coach, what exactly are we playing today?

Coach: We're studying the Continental Congress.

Susan: Not again! My team always loses!

Thomas: Maybe this time will be different.

Coach: OK. Number off!

9 But It's NOT Sunday!

LESSON IN A NUTSHELL

In this lesson, each young person will examine the fullness of the Christian life and decide what he or she can and cannot do as a Christian.

BUT THIS IS THE SANCTUARY! (10–15 minutes)

Gather the group and head to your church's sanctuary. Remind the tweens that the sanctuary is the center of worship for your church community and that they are to view it with respect. Have the group look around the sanctuary. Give them several moments to walk around.

Gather the group together. Ask:

- Does this place feel different than it does on Sunday morning?

WHAT DAY IS BEST? (10–15 minutes)

Give everyone a copy of "What Day Is Best?" (page 38). Go over the instructions.

After everyone has had a chance to fill out his or her worksheet, have the group compare answers. Then ask:

- Why do some of the schedules look different from others?
- Is your schedule strict, or can you move some items around?
- Who determines what activities you will do each day?
- Why did you place "Pray" and "Read the Bible" where you did?

THE WEIGHT OF APPROVAL (5–10 minutes)

Here is a chance for each person to express his or her opinion on the certain topics. Everyone votes by moving to one side of the room or the other. Designate one side as "Agree" and one side as "Disagree." Everyone must move toward one side or the other on each issue, although he or she may indicate by where he or she stands how strongly he or she feels about the issue.

Before They Arrive

- ❑ Make enough copies of "What Day is Best?" (page 38) for each person.
- ❑ If possible, conduct the entire program in the sanctuary. Check with the church office to make sure it is available.

Supplies

- ❑ Bibles for all
- ❑ Pencils or pens

Some topics are

- Youth under 16 should not be allowed out after 8:00 p.m.
- Christians should be expected to be at worship every Sunday.
- Our police and our courts should be tougher on lawbreakers than they are.
- Violence is never an acceptable alternative for a Christian.
- There are times when it is OK to bend the truth.
- Family always comes before friends.

Gather the group together, then ask:

- When you moved to show your opinion, were you watching how others were voting to determine how to vote?

LOOK A LITTLE DEEPER (10–15 minutes)

Ask a volunteer to read aloud **Mark 2:23-28.** Ask:

- What was Jesus doing that was "not lawful"?
- How did he respond?
- Did Jesus believe that the Sabbath was a day different from any other day? Why, or why not?

Say: **The Sabbath was meant to be a time of rest and reflection for the faithful of God. It had become much more than that by Jesus' time. The Sabbath had become a strictly controlled day in which people were to limit their actions.**

Ask:

- Do we treat Sunday as a Sabbath?
- If so, do we use it in the way Jesus described it or in the way the authorities enforced it?
- What does it really mean to be a Christian?

Say: **In an earlier exercise, we visually demonstrated our opinions on a number of topics. Our opinions might change, based on how much we know about a subject, what we have experienced, or how we perceive others think. As Christians, we are to consider one more factor: what we believe God wants.**

When Time Matters

If you have more time:

Obtain copies of *Pockets* (or another tween or youth devotional) and hand those out to the group. Explain to the tweens how a devotional works (walking them through one), and encourage them to use it during the week.

To order copies of *Pockets*, call Upper Room customer service toll-free at 800-925-6847.

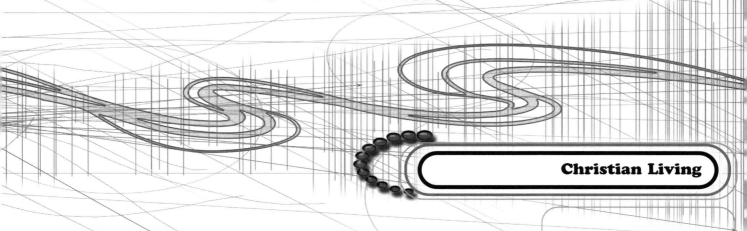

SENDING FORTH (2–5 minutes)

Ask the group to look at the "What Day Is Best?" worksheets again.

Say: **Look at your sample weekly calendar. If Christians are called to follow God every day, that would mean that prayer and Bible study are not limited to just Sunday. This week, spend at least a few minutes in prayer each day. Use this or another schedule as a guide. As you look at your schedule, ask God how you may be a more faithful follower through each activity. Remember, prayer is also about listening; so listen to what God may be saying to you.**

Pray as a group. Start the prayer by asking God to prepare everyone's hearts and minds to hear God. Allow others to pray as they feel lead.

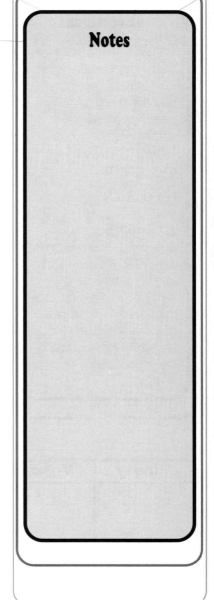

Notes

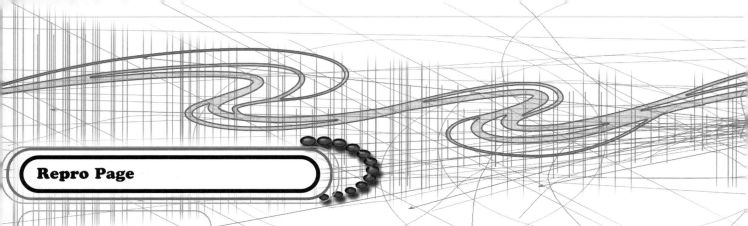

What Day Is Best?

Directions

Write in the space next to the activity the best (or most appropriate) day (or days) of the week to do each activity. Add any other weekly activities you might have.

Circle any activities that are a part of your actual weekly routine and write them in the calendar. If you do the activity every day, write it on the first day you do it, then just draw a line from that day through all of the days you do it.

_____ Go to school.

_____ Ride a bike.

_____ Study.

_____ Go to the zoo.

_____ Pray.

_____ Spend the night at a friend's house.

_____ Play soccer or another sport.

_____ See a movie at a theater.

_____ Read the Bible.

_____ Help with household chores.

_____

_____

_____

_____

Sunday	Monday	Tuesday	Wednesday	Thursday	Friday	Saturday

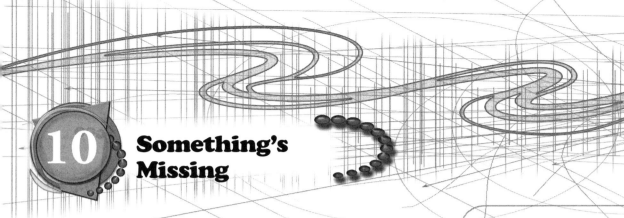

10 Something's Missing

LESSON IN A NUTSHELL

This lesson is designed to help everyone work together while learning to take responsibility for his or her own faith.

WHO I AM IS WHAT I LIKE (10–15 minutes)

As tweens arrive, have them write their name on one side of a sheet of paper and draw a picture of their favorite hobby, favorite place, and favorite food item on the other side. These can be as intricate or simple as they want. Let them know that other people will have to guess who drew the pictures based on these items, so they may want to keep their pictures secret until it is time to guess. Have them keep adding details to their pictures until everyone is ready.

Collect the pictures and hold them up one at a time for people to guess the identity of the artist. If the group doesn't know one another's names yet, have those written on a list (such as a chalkboard) for everyone to see. Have the tweens guess each artist before you reveal the true identity.

After everyone's art is identified, have the group post their pictures on the wall or a bulletin board, or attach them to a big sheet of butcher paper to make a quick mural.

SOMETHING'S MISSING (10–15 minutes)

Have the tweens look around the room to see if they can spot what's missing. Ask them to brainstorm what the room needs that isn't there. Encourage them to search the room and to discuss with one another what might be missing. Have them make a list on a markerboard or paper of what they think is missing.

Next, tell them what you actually did remove and where you put it. Give them a general sense, such as "still in this room" or "on this side of the sanctuary." Let them find these items and bring them back to the room.

Afterward, give everyone a copy of "Something's Missing" (page 41) to do. Go over the answers when the tweens are ready. Affirm their knowledge and cooperation.

Before They Arrive

❑ Make enough copies of "Something's Missing" (page 41) for each person, including adults. Also, make sure that the room is missing an object or two that the group might expect to see (such as a table, Bibles, or a favorite poster if they know the room well).

Supplies

❑ Bibles for all
❑ Paper and colored pencils or markers
❑ Pens or pencils

Answers to page 41

1. penny/penny
2. 15
3. blue
4. wine
5. 12
6. Moses
7–10. (Answers will vary.)

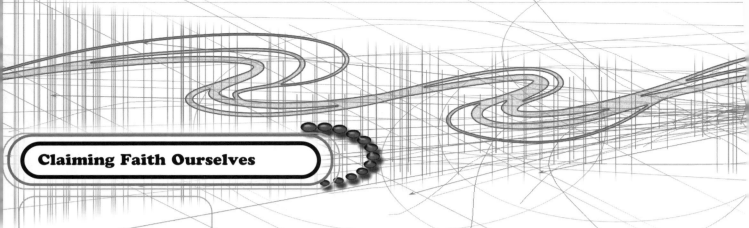

Claiming Faith Ourselves

When Time Matters

If you have less time:

"Who I Am Is What I Like"—Have each person draw just one picture.

"Something's Missing"—Hide whatever is missing in the room and bring it out when they identify it.

If you have more time:

Play a game of "Spot the Change." Have everyone pair off. (Ask an adult to play or sit out as necessary to complete the pairs.) Each pair must stand face-to-face and look at each other for 30 seconds. Then they must turn back-to-back and change one thing about their appearance. Bring them back face-to-face and ask them to spot the change in their partner. Mix up each pair and do it again. Play as long as you'd like.

LOOK A LITTLE DEEPER (10–20 minutes)

Be sure to let the group know that we will be building on the first few lessons. Tell them how important it is that they attend regularly and participate actively.

Ask someone who reads well to read **Luke 2:41-52,** and have everyone else try to imagine the scene. If there is time, also have volunteers act out the drama silently or with dialogue. After the reading, remind the group that Jesus was twelve when this happened—about the same age as most of the group. Ask:

- What did you find new or surprising about this story?
- Why did Jesus stay behind in the Temple? Was he being disobedient?
- What would happen if you stayed behind like that? How would you explain yourself?
- What did Jesus say in verse 49 that his parents didn't understand? What do you think he meant?
- Parents provide for us in so many ways. Are there any responsibilities you have already taken on for yourself (such as doing your own laundry)?
- What are some responsibilities you find it hard to take on for yourself?
- What is scary or challenging about leaving childhood? How can you face it?

Say: **Jesus wasn't being disobedient. He simply knew that he had a higher purpose and that he wouldn't be a child much longer. So, too, is it with you. While you do not have to become adults just yet, you are at a point at which you need to take responsibility for your own emotions, relationships, and spirituality. Jesus was still obedient to his parents (verse 51); he also accepted responsibility for his own faith.**

That's what we are called to do, as well. You are changing from children and becoming more grown up. Nothing will ever be the same as it was, but nothing has to be missing. Instead, we can claim our own faith and know God for ourselves. Faith isn't something that comes easy, but it is something that will be there for us if we look for it. While our lives may change, we know that we can always have our faith and our God. And we can have one another as you make this change.

SENDING FORTH (2–5 minutes)

Have everyone form a circle. Tell the participants that you will soon begin a prayer. Go around the circle and ask them to each mention someone by name who is important to them. Let them know that it is OK to just say "Mom" or "Dad" or some other simple title if they would like. Begin the prayer by asking God to help everyone as they claim their faith for themselves. Pray as a group.

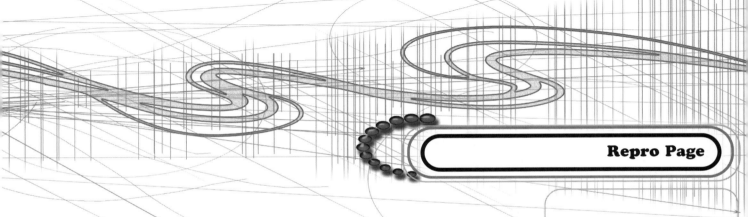

Something's Missing

1. "A _____ saved is a _____ earned."

2. $42 + 42 + \_\_\_ = 99$

3. Mixing yellow paint and _____ paint creates green paint.

4. Jesus turned water into _____ at a wedding.

5. Peter was one of the _____ (a number) disciples.

6. _____ and his brother, Aaron, led the Hebrews out of Egypt.

7. _____ has the most brothers and sisters in our group.

8. _____ traveled the longest to get here.

9. _____ (member of our group) has the longest full name (first, middle, last).

10. _____ can name the first five New Testament books.

Directions

Take a few moments to decide what is missing from the statements at left. You might need the help of others to complete some of these statements.

11 Yesterday, Today, & Tomorrow

Before They Arrive

❑ Make enough copies of "Yesterday, Today, & Tomorrow" (page 44) for each person.

Supplies

❑ Bibles for all
❑ Several newspapers and/or periodicals (They should be somewhat current but can be a few weeks old.)
❑ Scissors
❑ Glue
❑ Large sheets of construction paper
❑ Large sheets of paper
❑ Markers
❑ Cotton balls (optional)
❑ Watercolor paints and brushes and clean-up materials (optional)
❑ Glitter (optional)
❑ Other creative "cloud-making" supplies (optional)

LESSON IN A NUTSHELL

This lesson is designed to give to each person assurance of God's presence.

WHERE IS GOD TODAY? (10–15 minutes)

Spread out several newspapers or other periodicals for the tweens to use to make collages. Tell the group that they are to find examples of God's presence in the world today. They may also find examples that suggest God may not be present in the world today.

Have them mount their findings on construction paper. Then have them show and talk about their collage with the entire group.

YESTERDAY, TODAY, & TOMORROW (10–15 minutes)

Give each tween a copy of "Yesterday, Today, & Tomorrow" (page 44). Go over the instructions with them. Ask:

- What do the passages say about the nature of God?
- What do they say about those who believe in God?

HOW CAN I KNOW THAT GOD IS HERE? (15–25 minutes)

Divide the tweens into smaller groups of three or four. Ask them to come up with examples of Bible people, historical people, and contemporary people whose lives show God's presence. The contemporary examples may be parents or other family members, friends or other people they know personally, or people they may know about through the media.

Have the groups tell the stories of the people they selected and how those persons' lives showed God's presence. Then ask:

- How can I know that God is with me?

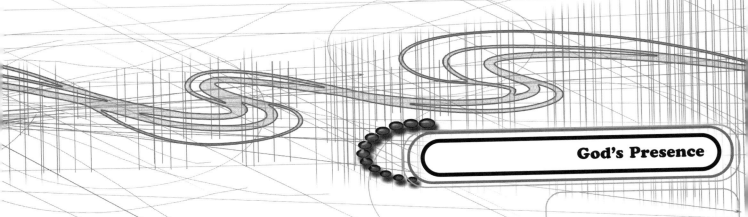

LOOK A LITTLE DEEPER (10–20 minutes)

Have a volunteer read aloud **Hebrews 12:1.** Talk about the fact that the stories the tweens have just told are of people who have witnessed to us about God's presence in the world. They become a "cloud of witnesses" for us.

Have the tweens in their small groups create a large "cloud" and write on the cloud the names of the people (biblical, historical, and contemporary) whose stories they told. They may choose from the various art supplies how to create their cloud. Once they have completed their cloud, they can post it on the wall with the others.

Invite the tweens to tell their own stories of experiences they have had that reassured them of God's presence. Then have them write their own names on their clouds.

SENDING FORTH (2–5 minutes)

Have everyone form a circle. If your group is completing a cycle of several of the other lessons in this book, remark on what you have accomplished together during the past weeks.

Read aloud **Hebrews 12:1** again.

Say: **We are all on a journey, a "race that is set before us," We do not know what is before us. But the witness of all these people, and your own experience, tells us that God is with us no matter what.**

In our prayer time, we will pray for one another.

Go around the circle, praying aloud for each tween, asking that he or she be aware of and rely upon God's presence in the days ahead.

When Time Matters

If you have more time:

"Where Is God Today?"—
Have the tweens use the Internet to search for even more accounts of how God is acting in the world today.

Caution: Never allow tweens to visit a website unless you know that it is a good site. Be careful of names similar to those to good sites. They may have been chosen to deceive you into visiting a less than reputable site.

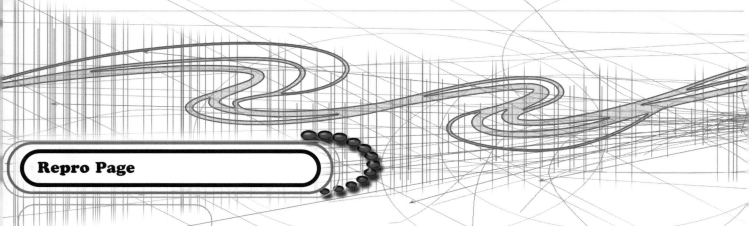

Yesterday, Today, & Tomorrow

Directions

Look up each of the verses at right. What do they say to you about the nature of God?

What other verses can you add about God? Add them below the others.

Genesis 1:1-2 _____

Exodus 3:13-15 _____

Psalm 90:1-2 _____

Psalm 145:13-14 _____

John 1:1-5 _____

John 3:16-17 _____

Hebrews 13:8 _____

Revelation 22:13 _____

_____ _____

_____ _____

_____ _____

12 Why Should I Care?

LESSON IN A NUTSHELL

This lesson examines the role of the Christian in viewing others as people of worth who are precious to God.

COOKING (30–60 minutes)

As soon as people start arriving (or maybe sooner, if you choose a different meal), begin fixing dinner. Invite everyone to hang out in the kitchen and dining areas and talk with one another while the food is cooking.

Assign various tasks to the tweens. Have adult supervision, as necessary (such as when a tween is slicing tomatoes). Remember to have someone set the tables (complete with paper placemats) as well.

When the meal is ready, seat the main cooks first and have other members of the group serve them dinner. Make sure that everyone has a chance to participate.

Have the tweens clear the tables of everything, except the placemats and distribute markers, pencils, or pens and Bibles to everyone.

CONCERNS (2–5 minutes)

Have everyone turn over his or her placemat even if it is soiled.

Say: **Every one of us has fears, concerns, and problems. Take a moment to think about your fears, concerns, and problems. Write down a particular concern of yours on one part of your placemat.**

Now, think of a problem or fear that you do not have, but someone else may have. For instance, while we have had a good meal, many people do not get enough food to eat. Write down on your placemat a concern that you think someone else has.

Before They Arrive

❑ Arrange to have a kitchen and all of the supplies necessary to cook a meal together.
❑ Contact the tweens' parents for help providing the food. (Your call will also ensure good attendance for the meal.)
❑ The menu should be something filling, yet simple, that more than one person can work on at a time, without a lot of focus on the cooking, such as: Spaghetti with sauce, garlic bread, salad, and a drink; OR Tacos (shells, meat, cheese, garnish), rice, refried beans, and a drink.

Supplies

❑ Bibles for all
❑ Dinner ingredients
❑ Plates, utensils, cups, napkins, and so on
❑ Paper placemats (to be used in the program)
❑ Enough pocket crosses, coins (preferably shiny and distinctive), or other pocket-sized momentoes to distribute during worship
❑ Markers, pencils, or pens (Do not use markers if the table has a fabric tablecloth on it, as the ink might soak through.)

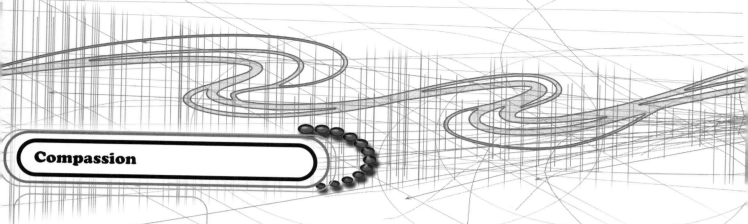

Compassion

BUT THEY DON'T COUNT! (10–15 minutes)

Ask the group to come up with a definition of *compassion* (*a deep awareness of the suffering of another and a desire to relieve it*). Then have them think of some examples.

Say: **God calls us to show compassion for everyone, because everyone is loved by God. Surely there are exceptions, right? On another part of your placemat write down the names of some people or groups that you think do not deserve compassion.**

Divide the tweens into small groups at their tables and assign the following passages to different groups to read and discuss in light of their lists they just made: **Genesis 6:1-8; Jonah 4; Matthew 5:43-48; John 3.**

Invite each small group to report on their passage and their conversation. Affirm their efforts. Ask the whole group:

- Does this information change your view on any of the above groups? How?

LOOK A LITTLE DEEPER (10–15 minutes)

Ask some tweens to take turns reading aloud from **Matthew 25:31-46.** Ask:

- Who does Jesus say will have shown him compassion?
- As you think about the people we've just identified, what are some ways to show them compassion?
- What are some of the barriers or fears that keep us from showing compassion? How might we overcome them?
- Why should we care about anyone but ourselves?

Have the tweens each pick up their placemat and crumple it. Pass a trash can or bag from tween to tween for them to put the crumpled placemats in.

Say: **Just like throwing away the placemats, it would be easy to let the concerns and problems of others disappear from our minds. But as Christians, we ask ourselves, How can these problems be addressed if we forget they exist?**

Have the tweens finish cleaning up and then gather as a group for the Sending Forth.

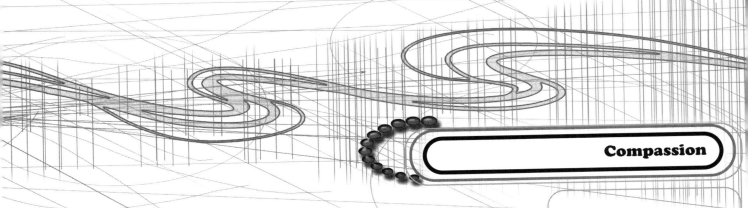

SENDING FORTH (2–5 minutes)

Say: **It is easy to forget the concerns of others. It is especially easy to ignore people who might be lonely or hurting. We are all guilty of turning away from those who need us. Let's each pray silently and confess our failures to God.**

Allow time for silent prayer and then continue.

Say: **One way we show compassion is through our prayers. Let us offer up prayers on behalf of the people we know who are in need.**

Invite the group to name people or groups of people to pray for. Pray together.

Show everyone the coins, crosses, or other pocket-sized trinkets.

Say: **This will serve as a reminder to reach out to others. God will show you ways to help. Always remember that others are human beings, just as you are, and loved by God, just as you are.**

As each person steps forward, hand him or her the item.

Say: **"As you have done unto the least of these, so have you done it unto me." Amen.**

The Concept of Compassion

While service is the focus of the second half of this book, the concept of "compassion" is impossible to understand without some experience of service.

Provide your group with an an opportunity to take their learnings in this session and turn it into service for others. Encourage the ideas for service to come from the group.

Refer to the second half of this book for additional ideas.

Service Programs

1 Neighbor to Neighbor

LESSON IN A NUTSHELL

An expert in the Law once asked Jesus, "Who is my neighbor?" This project will help tweens answer this question for themselves. In a gesture of neighborliness, the tweens will go door to door, delivering free carnations and newspapers to neighborhood residents.

DISCOVERING THE NEED

Many people live in isolation or have little sense of being known and cared about by persons who are in their neighborhoods. They long for contact from someone who cares. This project will allow your tweens to be that loving contact—a neighbor who truly cares.

A map of your community will help you determine the neighborhoods to visit. If possible, visit apartments and homes closest to your church. If your facility is not close to a residential neighborhood, ask your pastor for suggestions.

Something to Consider

Door-to-door outreach can have a significant impact on those homes and apartments closest to your church. With a mixture of surprise, anger, or frustration, church neighbors will frequently make comments like this one:

"This is the first time a church (or your church) has ever bothered to visit us."

This type of project can begin to tear down walls and build much-needed bridges. You can seen hardened hearts soften during this simple outreach project.

The Gift of Neighbors

What You Will Need

Buy or have the participants bring these supplies:

❑ Carnations
❑ Stack of today's newspapers
❑ Other items (See Getting Ready for more suggestions.)

Considerations

People are often skeptical of door-to-door solicitors. Make it clear that you are giving away carnations and papers—not selling them. These neighborly gifts from the tweens come with "no strings attached."

Don't accept donations. If they insist on making one, have them mail a check to the church. You are giving a gift of love—not doing a fundraiser.

GETTING READY

❑ Select the neighborhoods you would like to contact.
❑ Determine what items to take—newspapers, carnations, small plants in pots, loaf of bread, fresh-baked cookies, daffodil or tulip bulbs, helium-filled balloons, seed packets, smoke detector batteries, bottled water, cold canned or bottled drinks, hot coffee or something else. Keep it simple. Just choose one or two items.
❑ Determine when your event will take place (Sunday morning, late Sunday afternoon, or another time during the week). If you choose Sunday morning, consider taking toaster tarts, fresh donuts, fresh brewed coffee, orange juice, breakfast burritos, or another morning goody.
❑ Make your local police department aware of your project. If they receive any calls, they will already know what you are doing.
❑ Enlist enough chaperones. You will need one chaperone for every four to five tweens.
❑ Determine how many carnations and papers you will need, based on the number of homes to be visited.
❑ Call your local florists and newspaper publisher. They may provide items "at cost" or free.
❑ Prepare travel permission forms for each tween (to be signed by a parent or guardian).

GATHER 'N' GAB (10–15 minutes)

As the tweens arrive, have them divide the items evenly among the teams. Talk briefly about the event and schedule. Share tips and safety concerns. Answer questions. Be sure to read aloud Special Tips (in the margin on page 51.)

GOD'S WORD (10–15 minutes)

Have someone read aloud **Luke 10:25-37** (the good Samaritan). Ask:

- Who are your neighbors?
- Are they friendly? Do you know their names? How long have they been your next door neighbors?
- Name someone who isn't your neighbor?
- What does the Bible tells us about who our neighbors are?

Say: **Today's Bible passage gives a broad understanding of the word neighbors. Neighbors are more than those who live next door. Everyone is your neighbor. And we are invited by Christ to demonstrate God's love to them.**

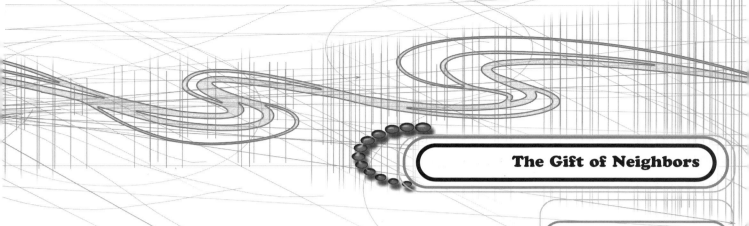

Pray: **Dear God, bless us as we reach out in love to our neighbors. Amen.**

TWEENS IN MISSION (60–90 minutes)

Your checklist:

❑ Gather your supplies and count everyone.
❑ Remind the tweens of safety concerns; and make final instructions.
❑ Have the tweens help load the supplies.
❑ Make sure that they have a clear understanding of what they are doing and why.
❑ Remind them of the time limit and where to meet afterward.
❑ Each group will need a spokesperson.
❑ Your spokesperson should say something like: "We are delivering free carnations and newspapers to our neighbors. Would you like one?" See the note on Considerations (in the margin on page 50).
❑ Count everyone. Return to the church on/before the time limit.

SNACK 'N' YACK (20–35 minutes)

Serve snacks and refreshments. Find a comfortable location for debriefing. If you had multiple groups visiting, have each one describe for the others where they went and what the experience was like. Ask:

- How did our neighbors respond to our kindness?
- How did today's experience make you feel?
- Did you enjoy this project? Why, or why not?
- What did today's devotional have to do with what we did?

If you intend to have the group repeat this project at another time, ask:

- Are there other neighborhoods we should visit? What should we take those neighbors?
- Should we take carnations to mothers and grandmothers on Mother's Day?
- Can you think of other creative things we can do for our neighbors?

SENDING FORTH (2–5 minutes)

Pray: **Dear God, help us be faithful in sharing your love to everyone in need. May we see the world as you do—that everyone is our neighbor. Amen.**

Special Tips

- Don't visit too early or late.
- Divide into groups of five to six. However, only two or three people should go to each door. Don't overwhelm people with a large group.
- Don't allow anyone to visit alone, and don't go inside.
- Smile, be friendly, and respect their wishes. If they're not interested, say thank you and move on.
- Prepare to explain what you're doing. (They will ask.)
- Don't leave items outside the door. The wind, bad weather, or an animal could transform your gift into a litter problem.
- Stay alert for mean dogs, "keep out" or "no solicitors" signs, unsafe porches or steps, and other hazards.
- Be kind to rude people. Don't get into debates.
- If you discover someone who needs to talk, refer him or her to your pastor.
- Your visit shouldn't last over three to five minutes. Don't overstay your welcome.
- Don't take photographs unless you have consent.

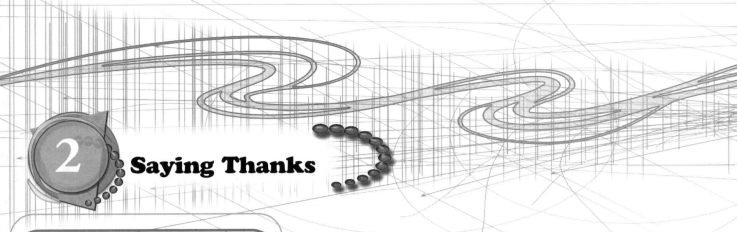

2 Saying Thanks

Something to Consider

The tweens of St. Mark United Methodist Church, Cleburne, Texas, takes snacks, homemade goodies, cold soft drinks to their fire departments each year.

Shortly after the tragedies of September 11, 2001, they made a special trip. The group made and gave the firefighters friendship bracelets.

Accompanied by a guitar, everyone sang praise choruses by candlelight. In the twilight, the candlelight was breathtaking.

Moved by the tweens' gift, several of the firefighters stood crying; many of the tweens and their leaders did too.

LESSON IN A NUTSHELL

The biblical injunction to "outdo one another in showing honor" is something your tweens can do. Countless everyday heroes in your community deserve honor and respect. The tweens will deliver snacks and drinks to your local fire, police, and emergency medical teams.

DISCOVERING THE NEED

The events of September 11, 2001, have made us aware of the sacrifice our police, fire, and EMT personnel make each day. On a routine day, they will place their lives on the line for the safety and comfort of others. This project will honor those who protect, defend, and serve your community.

Your local phone book, city hall ,or community website should provide you with the telephone numbers and addresses you will need for this project. Gather pertinent information about the main stations and substations.

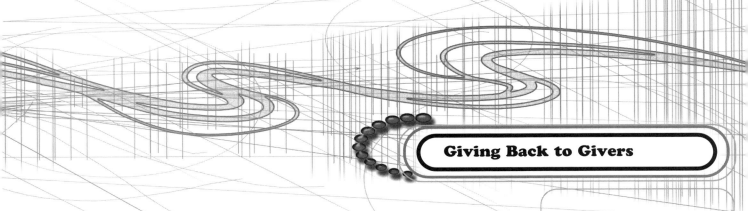

GETTING READY

❑ Depending on time constraints and material resources, you may need to limit the number of stops you make. If necessary, you can focus on one department (for example, fire, police, or EMT) and visit the others on a later date.

❑ Call each location ahead of time to let them know that your group plans to visit. Calling ahead is very important. Your police department, in particular, will appreciate the advance notice for security reasons.

❑ When you call, see if it is also possible for the department to give your tweens a short tour of their facility.

❑ Enlist enough drivers to help with transportation.

❑ Be sure to have signed permission slips from parents and guardians.

GATHER 'N' GAB (10–15 minutes)

As the tweens arrive, have them sort the items into delivery routes. Talk to them briefly about the schedule and the nature of the project. Answer questions.

Ask if any of them have ever experienced the help of these men and women who serve and protect the community. Allow them to tell their stories.

GOD'S WORD (10–15 minutes)

Have someone read aloud Romans 12:9-13 (show honor).

- Have you ever been honored for something? Perfect attendance? Grades? Spelling bee? Science project? Athletic event? A special achievement?
- How did it make you feel to be honored?
- What does it mean to honor someone? Other words for *honor* are *respect*, *revere*, *salute*, or *to pay tribute*.

Say: **Today (tonight) we will honor persons who protect, defend, and serve our community. It's our way of paying tribute for all they do.**

Pray: **Dear God, please protect those who protect, defend, and serve our community. As we honor them, may they feel special, appreciated, and truly blessed. Amen.**

What You Will Need

❑ Homemade treats
❑ Packages of snacks
❑ Large bags of chips
❑ Cans or bottles of soft drinks (or 2-liter bottles)
❑ Gum and individually wrapped candy
❑ Fruit and sugar-free items
❑ Ice chest and ice
❑ Extra drinks and snacks for the tweens to enjoy later
❑ Camera, preferably digital or instant

Considerations

Some groups may desire to make homemade brownies, cookies, and/or lemonade at the church. Others will simply want to bring store-bought items.

Special Tips

- Be sure to call the fire station and EMTs just before you leave. You may need to alter your schedule if they are leaving on an emergency run.
- Take plenty drinks and goodies for all of the personnel. In your initial call, ask how many people to prepare for.
- If it is inconvenient to take a cooler of iced drinks. Two-liter bottles work well too.
- It probably will not be necessary to take napkins, cups, or plates. The station should already have these items. To be certain, simply ask about this matter when you call.

TWEENS IN MISSION (60–90 minutes)

- Gather supplies and count everyone.
- Call each of the locations before you leave.
- Encourage the tweens to help load the supplies.
- Brief them on the location(s) to be visited. Make sure that the tweens have a clear understanding of what they are doing and why.
- Remind everyone of the time limit and where to meet afterward.
- If your group will be splitting up to go to more than one location, make sure that each group has a spokesperson, preferably a tween.
- Count everyone and board the vehicles.
- Upon arriving at the firehouse or police station, the spokesperson should introduce himself or herself and the group and explain the nature of the visit.
- If time allows, stay for a tour of the facility and questions and answers.
- Before leaving the station, ask permission to take some pictures of the tweens with the people they are honoring. Tell the personnel that the pictures will be on display in the tweens' gathering place. The pictures will be a reminder of this day and a way for the tweens to continue to honor and pray for these community servants.
- Count everyone. Return to the church on or before the time limit.

SNACK 'N' YACK (20–35 minutes)

Serve refreshments. Find a comfortable location for debriefing. Invite the tweens to describe the places and people they met. If the pictures taken are instant or digital, pass them around for the tweens to see again.

Ask:

- How did the men and women respond to your gifts?
- How did today's experience make you feel?
- Did you enjoy this project? Why, or why not?
- Where shall we display these photographs? (Some of the tweens may want to take some of photographs home, making a commitment to pray for the men and women they met for a specified time.)
- Did today's devotional relate to what we did? If yes, how?
- Are there other people or groups we should honor? If yes, whom should we honor? Why? When?

SENDING FORTH (2–5 minutes)

Pray: **Dear God, help us always honor those around us. May they sense our love and appreciation by the things we say and do. Amen.**

Tween Time

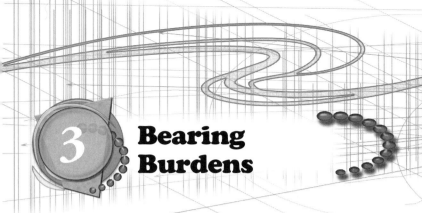

3 Bearing Burdens

LESSON IN A NUTSHELL

The tweens will discuss the expectations that Jesus has for Christians to be in service to those in need. They will collect teddy bears that will attend worship for several weeks prior to being delivered to a police station, fire department, or women's shelter to comfort scared children.

DISCOVERING THE NEED

Children in distress need a sense of security. Stuffed animals give children something tangible to hold on to, as well as a message that someone cares.

Check with your local police department, fire department, or women's shelter to see whether they could use teddy bears for comforting children in crisis. If they do not currently do so in such situations, you might suggest a pilot project in which you provide the teddy bears.

Something to Consider

The congregation of Bellevue United Methodist Church, in Nashville, Tennessee, has invited teddy bears into their congregation two times a year. On Teddy Bear Sunday, people bring bears to the sanctuary. The bears sit in the pews for three weeks so that people can love on them.

Then they are delivered to the local police department. When the police are in crisis situations in which children are involved, giving them a "loved on" teddy bear can ease their fears.

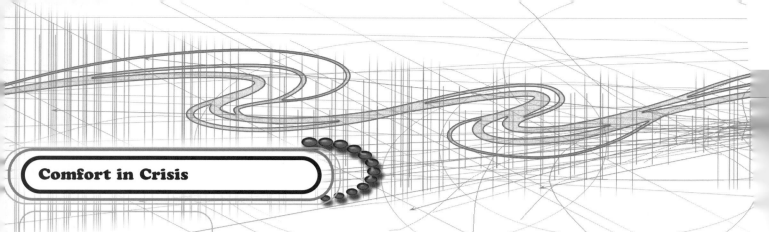

Comfort in Crisis

What You Will Need

- ❑ Teddy bears
- ❑ Ribbon or yarn
- ❑ Card stock (blank index cards work well)
- ❑ Paper punch
- ❑ Markers
- ❑ Stickers
- ❑ Laminating machine or clear self-adhesive plastic

Special Tips

Make more tags than the number of teddy bears currently in hand. As the project gains momentum in the congregation, more bears will come.

If you are in a bilingual community, include additional languages on the tags.

GET READY

- ❑ Contact the police or fire department or women's shelter.
- ❑ Check with your pastor and worship committee for approval to have teddy bears in the pews for two or three weeks.
- ❑ Place a notice in the bulletin and newsletter, requesting donations of **new** teddy bears 12–15 inches in size. (This size has been found to be the best.) A sample of the correct size teddy bear may be helpful for some people.
- ❑ Invite a representative of the agency who will receive the bears to come to your meeting to tell how the bears will be used.
- ❑ Gather the necessary supplies.

GATHER 'N' GAB (10–15 minutes)

As the tweens arrive, have them construct tags to attach to each teddy bear. The tags should be 3-by-5 inches. On the front of the tag write: "This bear has been held and loved by the members of (*insert the name of your church*). This bear brings our love to you." The tweens may decorate the tags with stickers after writing if there is room. Laminate the tags and punch a hole in one end. Secure a tag to each bear.

Have the tweens gather to hear the representative from the agency who will be receiving the bears. Be sure to thank the representative for coming.

Gather the tweens into small groups with an adult or older youth leader. Lead the tweens in a discussion based on the information provided by the agency representative. Include the following types of questions:

- ▪ How can teddy bears be helpful to this agency?
- ▪ Have you ever been in a crisis situation where you needed to feel loved?
- ▪ Whom would you trust if you felt abandoned and unloved?

GOD'S WORD (10–15 minutes)

Have volunteer tweens read aloud the following Scripture lessons:

John 13:34-35 (Love one another.)
1 John 3:18 (Show love through action.)

Have the tweens look up the word **love** in a concordance. Ask them to note the number of times that word is used in the New Testament. Have each tween look up a different Scripture and read it to the group.

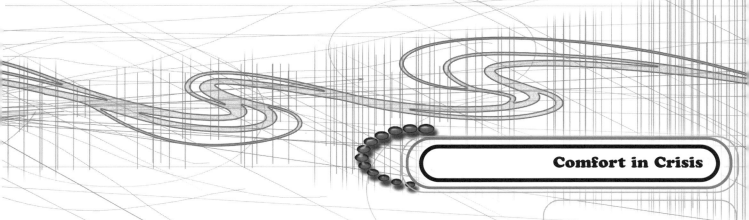

Lead the tweens in a discussion of the Scripture using the information below.

The Greek word *agape* is generally translated into the English word *love*. Living out the command to "love one another as Christ has loved" was the hallmark of the early Christian community. Christianity grew because people could see the love among Christians and from Christians to others. When individuals have a relationship with God, their attitude and actions give witness to that relationship.

Invite the tweens to talk about how they see God through the actions of others. Help them identify acts of kindness and compassion they have experienced or observed. Ask them also to think of situations where they could show kindness or compassion to someone else.

Pray: **Dear God, we often fail to act with love toward one another and those in need. Help us to be faithful disciples by showing love through our actions. Amen.**

TWEENS IN MISSION (1–2 hours)

Have the tweens gather around the prepared teddy bears. Invite the tweens to each hold a bear as you pray.

Pray: **Dear God, thank you for sending Jesus to show us how to care for one another. These bears will be joining us in worship for the next few weeks. May they help our congregation remember children who need to be comforted. May the children who receive these bears know your love. Amen.**

As a group, take the bears to the sanctuary and place them on pews. Be sure to place them throughout the entire sanctuary.

After you return to your meeting place, have the tweens gather in small groups. Have one group write an article for the newsletter, explaining the Bearing Burdens project. Have one group write an announcement for the bulletin. Have another group prepare a skit or announcement to be presented in worship the following Sunday to share the Bearing Burdens project with the congregation.

A Multiple-Week Project

Consider this schedule option for involving the congregation more:

Week 1

Introduce the project, with a guest speaker and the Bible study.

The tweens prepare announcements, newsletter articles, and skit for worship.

Week 2

The tweens make the tags for the bears.

The tweens continue to publicize the project.

Week 3

The tweens add tags and place the new bears in the pews.

Week 4

The tweens dedicate the bears; pray for the children who will receive them.

The tweens or designated persons take the bears to the agency.

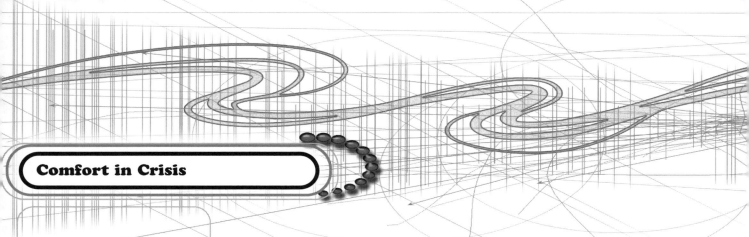

Comfort in Crisis

Notes

SNACK 'N' YACK (15–20 minutes)

Gather the tweens into small groups. Lead the them in a discussion of their experience of holding and praying over the teddy bears. Use the following or similar questions in your discussion.

- What do you do when you are lonely or afraid?
- Have you ever needed a hug when no one was around?
- Do you have a favorite stuffed animal?
- Where do you go when you need to feel closer to God?
- How do you think the congregation will respond to teddy bears in the pews?

SENDING FORTH (2–5 minutes)

Say: **Today we learned of the need for Christians to care for one another. By providing bears for children in crisis, we have responded to the needs of others.**

Let's pray that God will be with these children and with those who care for them.

Before we close in prayer, you may share your concerns for yourself, your family, or others so they may be lifted to God in prayer.

Allow each tween to write their concerns on paper so they may be included in the closing prayer. Invite one of the tweens to lead the closing prayer printed below:

Pray: **Dear God, help us to be aware of others in need. Help us to learn ways to care for each other. Be with those who receive these bears. We ask you to be with those we care about: (*read the prayer concerns here*). Thank you for hearing and responding to our needs. Amen.**

4 Healing Hearts

LESSON IN A NUTSHELL

The tweens will discuss the biblical concept of healing and discover how God uses everyday people to help bring healing. The tweens will make and deliver Healing Hearts Bags to the children, teens, or adults at a local healthcare facility.

DISCOVERING THE NEED

The role of emotional and prayer support in recovery is well documented. The tweens' visits and gifts can help deliver both.

What agencies in your area provide healing for children, teens, or adults in physical or emotional need? Is there a children's hospital nearby? a nursing home? A visit to a family waiting room at a hospital is another option.

Something to Consider

Tweens are eager to be involved in the life of the church. How might today's visit be the spark of a church-wide ministry to the facility your group visited?

What other groups in your congregation might be involved in today's mission? Consider partnering with an adult Sunday school class or other group to set up a regular visitation schedule to the facility.

Helping Others Heal

What You Will Need

- ❑ **Bag Construction Supplies:** Construction paper, paper sacks with handles, heart-shaped stickers, adhesive bandages, card stock, paper punch, curly ribbon, pens, glue, several dice, index cards for questions
- ❑ **Suggested Bag Items:** Coloring books and crayons, storybooks, bookmarks, note cards, small games, playing cards, Bibles, devotional booklets

GET READY

- ❑ Make arrangements with a local healthcare facility to tour the facility and deliver bags or packets to the children, teens, or adults.
- ❑ Obtain a list of suggested items for the bags from the facility director.
- ❑ Gather the suggested items for the Healing Hearts Bags. (See Special Tips, page 61.)
- ❑ Be sure to have signed transportation permission forms.
- ❑ Purchase necessary supplies to make the bags.
- ❑ Create a heart-shaped pattern, approximately 4-by-4 inches. Some of the tweens will want to use the pattern; others will be comfortable with creating their own.

GATHER 'N' GAB (15–20 minutes)

As the tweens arrive, have them use the items provided to decorate the bags. Let them use the heart pattern to cut a large heart from colored paper and glue the heart to the front of the bag. Then have the tweens arrange the suggested items in the bag and use curly ribbon to attach a note card to the bag. The note card should include a prayer for the person who will receive the bag.

Gather the tweens into small groups, with an adult or older youth leader. Provide one die and one set of question cards to each group. Write on index cards the questions below and give one of the cards to each group.

The tweens will take turns rolling the die. They will answer the question that corresponds with the number rolled. Continue until everyone has had two or three turns to respond.

1. How many times have you been in the hospital?
2. How many broken bones have you had?
3. Do you know anyone who has an incurable disease or medical condition?
4. Do you know anyone who is involved in a healthcare job? What is his or her name?
5. Have you ever been in or seen a bad accident?
6. If you were going to work in a healthcare job, which one would you choose?

GOD'S WORD (10–15 minutes)

Have one of the tweens read aloud **2 Kings 5:1-19** (the healing of Namaan).

Ask open-ended questions to discuss the difference between physical and spiritual healing.

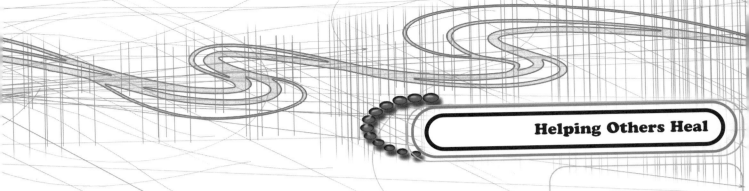

Ask the tweens to name other New Testament healing stories involving Jesus. These might include: **Matthew 9:27-29** (healing the blind men); **Mark 1:40-45** (healing the leper); **Mark 2:1-12** (healing the paralytic).

Ask open-ended questions about what they remember from these stories and how Jesus helps us understand the relationship between following Christ and healing.

Several important issues are raised in **2 Kings 5:1-19.** The servant girl's faith caused her to share that faith with Namaan's wife. King Aram had compassion for Namaan and was willing to spend a fortune to have him healed. The king of Israel seems unaware of Elisha's healing power. Namaan's strong will almost gets in the way of his healing. Healing can come from simple things. The servants' encouragement brings Namaan to follow through. Elisha takes no compensation for the healing. Namaan's attitude toward God changes.

Pray: **God, we can never fully understand your ways. Help us be instruments of healing. Show us how we can bring people closer to you. Amen.**

TWEENS IN MISSION (1–2 hours)

Say: **Today we will visit (***name of facility***) to learn how they provide for the physical and spiritual healing of the individuals in their care. We will provide spiritual healing by delivering our Healing Hearts Bags to the children, teens, or adults at the facility.**

Instruct the tweens to pay close attention to the caregivers at the facility and the way the patients respond to them.

SNACK 'N' YACK (15–20 minutes)

Gather the tweens into groups of four or five, with an adult or youth leader. Lead the tweens in a discussion of their visit by using the following or similar questions.

- Where did you see signs of healing?
- How did the patients respond to our visit?
- What does their response say about their healing experience?
- What were your thoughts or feelings during this visit?
- How did the patients respond to the healthcare providers?

Special Tips

To get the number and variety of the items for the bags, you may need to do some coordinating.

One option is to have each tween bring one of each of the items. However, be sensitive to financial issues.

Another option is to request dollar or item donations from congregation members and take the tweens shopping.

61

Tween Time

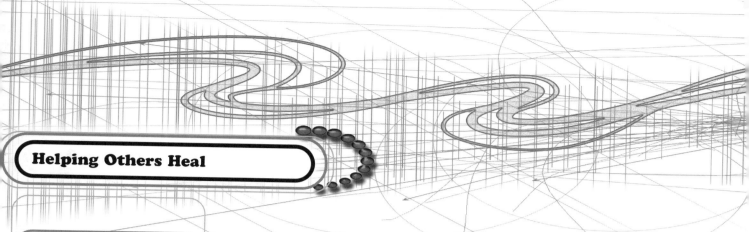

Notes

SENDING FORTH (2–5 minutes)

Say: **The concept of healing may be difficult for us to comprehend. Sometimes we fail to understand God's timing; and sometimes healing is not physical, but spiritual or within relationships. Today we had the opportunity to observe aspects of healing in action. And today we became instruments of spiritual healing.**

Before we close in prayer, you may share your concerns for yourself, your family, or others so that they may be lifted to God in prayer.

Encourage the tweens to write down prayer requests so they may be included in the closing prayer. Invite one of the tweens to lead the closing prayer below.

Pray: **Dear God, your love and mercy are bigger than we are. We do not understand how your healing power works. We lift up to you our concerns and praises. (*Read the list of concerns.*) Thank you for using us to be instruments of your healing presence to those we visited today. Amen.**

5 Sack Lunches

LESSON IN A NUTSHELL

The tweens will focus on compassion, as shown by Jesus and his disciples. As the tweens deliver free sack lunches to persons in impoverished apartment complexes or neighborhoods in your community, your tweens will experience compassion first hand.

DISCOVERING THE NEED

According to Bread for the World, 3.1 percent of U.S. households experience hunger; an even larger percentage experience a day-to-day insecurity about how they will get their next meal. That insecurity multiplies, especially at the end of pay periods, when the money is low or gone. Of necessity, these families frequently skip meals or eat too little, sometimes going without food for a whole day.

Where can you find the poor and hungry in your community? Where do the homeless and hungry congregate? Are there street corners or public places where they typically hang out? Are there any HUD, low-income, or sub-standard housing projects nearby? In other words, where would you find the pockets of poverty?

Something to Consider

In the summer of 1999, a junior high group in Cleburne, Texas, started just like this. As an act of compassion, they delivered 50 sack lunches one Saturday morning.

Today, they deliver 1,000 sack lunches each month to hungry families in North Texas.

Although it is impossible for your group to change the world, they can change the day for nearby hungry people. There's just no telling where your acts of compassion will lead. God bless you!

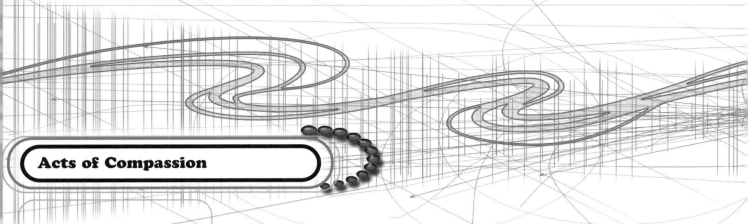

Acts of Compassion

What You Will Need

❏ Loaves of wheat bread
❏ Sliced ham and cheese
❏ Mustard (Squirt bottles are easier to use.)
❏ Large jar of pickles (hamburger slices)
❏ Zip-type bags (one for each sandwich)
❏ Individually wrapped cookies or pieces of fruit (one for each bag)
❏ Individually wrapped chips (one for each bag)
❏ Napkins (one for each bag)
❏ Paper lunch bags
❏ Markers in a variety of colors
❏ Optional: Gospel of John, a New Testament, or a devotional booklet for each bag
❏ Food service gloves and hairnets (recommended)
❏ Large crates or cardboard boxes (optional) for carrying filled bags

GET READY

❏ Your denominational offices for your area, as well as your local police department, may help you pinpoint the impoverished areas in town.
❏ You may also want to consult your United Way or other local care-giving agencies.
❏ Determine how many sack lunches you will deliver. Consider 25–50 as a maximum.
❏ Have travel permission forms for each tween.

GATHER 'N' GAB (10–15 minutes)

As the tweens arrive, have paper bags and markers available on tables. Ask the tweens to sit down and to have fun decorating each bag. Suggest that they also write encouraging comments such as "God loves you" or "Our church loves you," in addition to their creative Christian artwork.

As the group is working, tell them what you know about the place they will be visiting. This step is crucial. Providing a pre-trip briefing will help them understand the need, understand their role, and to have their fears and questions addressed.

GOD'S WORD (10–15 minutes)

Have one of the tweens read aloud **Matthew 15:32-33** (I do not want to send them away hungry). Then ask,

▪ What does it mean to have compassion?

Some of the tweens may say:

> Feeling sorry or sad
> Feeling guilty
> Having pity

Say: **Compassion is more than feeling sympathy. It is a sympathetic awareness of others' distress and something else.**

Invite the tweens to tell the rest of the story. What did Jesus do? What did the disciples do? What about the young boy (compare **Mark 8:1-10**)?

Say: **That "something else" is a willingness to do something about it. It is feeling the need, and acting upon it!**

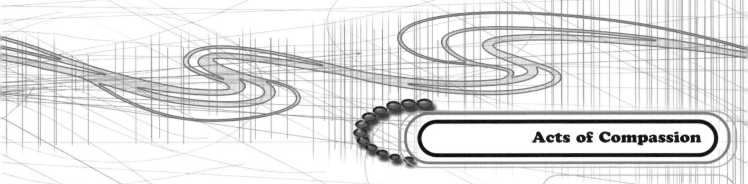

Point out that Jesus, the disciples, and the boy gave out of what they had— even though it didn't seem like enough. Tell the tweens that today they will have an opportunity to experience showing compassion first hand!

Pray: **God, help us be like the disciples and the young boy. But most of all, help us be more like your son, Jesus Christ. Give us hearts filled with compassion and the desire to do something special for others in need. Amen.**

TWEENS IN MISSION (60–90 minutes)

You will need
❏ One or two tables for sack lunch construction
❏ A separate table for supplies
❏ Another table to prepare and bag up the sandwiches

How to get started
❏ All participants need to wash their hands with soap and warm water.
❏ Have the group prepare the sandwiches first.
❏ Use an assembly line approach to assemble the sack lunches.
❏ Have the tweens prepare a lunch for themselves (to be eaten later)

Before you leave, form a circle and
❏ Explain proper behavior (see below) and the process of handing out the lunches (see below). It's easier to address these matters in the privacy of your church, rather than on site. Invite questions from the tweens.
❏ Be sure to pray as a group. Ask God to bless this day of compassion.
❏ You might want to divide the group into teams of three to five persons before leaving.

Proper behavior
• No pointing or staring
• No laughing, snickering, or making fun of people
• No horseplay with the sack lunches
• No "ring and run"
• No running off by yourself

How to distribute the lunches
❏ Three to five people should go to each home. Large crowds overwhelm the families.
❏ One person should be the designated spokesperson.

Special Tips
• Use mustard, not mayonnaise. Mayonnaise tends to spoil quicker.

• Use wheat, not white bread. White bread crushes easily.

• Use ham and cheese, not peanut butter and jelly. A lot of kids are allergic to peanuts!

• Use zip-type, not fold-over sandwich bags. They're easier to handle, and stay sealed better.

• Place pickles between the ham and cheese. Otherwise, the bread gets soggy.

• Putting the sandwich in last helps keep it from getting crushed.

• Do not let the sack lunches sit around; deliver them immediately.

• It's easier to transport your tweens and sack lunches in larger vehicles. SUVs and vans are recommended.

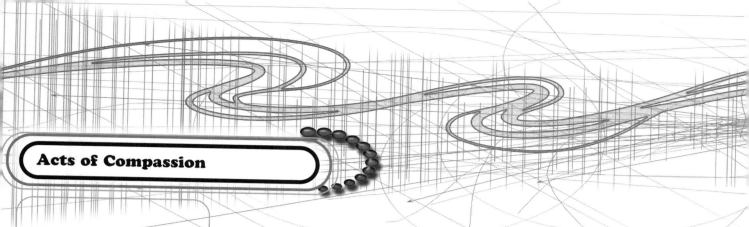

Acts of Compassion

Additional Information

If you would like more information about setting up a sack lunch ministry of your own, contact Mark Bushor at mbushor@yahoo.com.

❑ The spokesperson should say, "Hello, we are giving away free sack lunches and wondered whether you might like to have enough of them for your family." It is important to say the word *free*. Otherwise, they will think you are selling them.

❑ If the resident seems disinterested, simply go to the next apartment.

❑ Regardless of the residents' interest, leave, saying, "God bless you!"

SNACK 'N' YACK (15–30 minutes)

After you have distributed all of the free lunches, find a comfortable location where the tweens can enjoy their own sack lunch and talk freely about the activity. You can either return to the church or find a separate off-site location for this.

- Describe the homes and people we met today
- How did people respond to your help?
- How did today's experience make you feel?
- Did you enjoy helping other people?
- Did today's devotional relate to what we did? If yes, how?
- Has this experience changed your attitudes or ideas about poverty?
- What else would you like to do to help others?

SENDING FORTH: (2–5 minutes)

Pray: **Dear God, help us always live as your compassionate people. When we see a need, give us the desire and courage to reach out with your love. Amen.**

6 A BRIEF Blessing

LESSON IN A NUTSHELL

The prophet Isaiah once said:

"If you offer your food to the hungry and satisfy the needs of the afflicted, then your light shall rise in the darkness" (Isaiah 58:10).

In a world filled with darkness and despair, tweens can become a ray of light and a tangible expression of compassion. As agents of God's compassion, your tweens will collect packages of new underwear during the holiday season. Items collected may be given to a local agency for Christmastime distribution.

DISCOVERING THE NEED

A representative of Salvation Army once said:

"The poor and homeless are forced to do without the luxuries of life. Things like socks; mittens; and, especially, underwear fall into this category."

At Christmas, many people contribute to drives helping persons who are needy. However, one need that often gets overlooked is the need for basics such as underwear. Your local United Way, Salvation Army, elementary school counselor, or denominational office can help you locate a partner agency. Having a co-sponsor will allow you to concentrate on collecting items; your co-sponsor will be responsible for distribution.

Something to Consider

One group started by collecting 1,000 pairs of mittens at Christmastime. Now, in partnership with their local Salvation Army, they collect in excess of 5,000 pairs of underwear each fall.

On several occasions, Salvation Army representatives have said, "We depend on your young people to provide us with enough underwear for our Christmas baskets. We can't do it without you!"

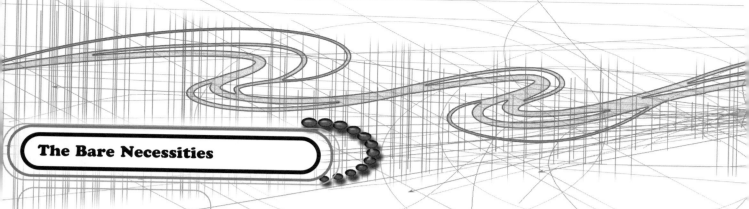

The Bare Necessities

What You Will Need

- ❏ Several extra-large cardboard boxes
- ❏ Christmas wrapping paper and wide ribbon (to wrap the boxes)
- ❏ Scissors and tape
- ❏ Supplies to make signs for the boxes
- ❏ Have the tweens bring $5.00 per person.

GET READY

- ❏ Select and contact an agency or school with similar goals and values to co-sponsor this project with your tweens.
- ❏ Contact your pastor to solicit her or his support, if necessary, to present the project to your church council or the appropriate group.
- ❏ Determine whether collection boxes will be placed throughout the community, in your church foyer, or both.
- ❏ Your co-partner agency will help you determine which items to collect—mittens, gloves, underwear, socks, and so on.
- ❏ Clarify expectations—what your church will do, what they will need to do.
- ❏ Determine the starting and finishing dates. Typically, you will begin collecting underwear just after Thanksgiving. But consider starting after Halloween and ending by Thanksgiving. That timeframe is close enough to Christmas without your project getting lost among numerous others.
- ❏ Place weekly "A BRIEF Blessing" announcements in the church newsletter and bulletin.
- ❏ Make "brief" announcements: "I would like to talk 'briefly' about. . . ."
- ❏ Place large collection receptacles in the narthex or in hallways. Decorate the receptacles as Christmas gift boxes and clearly mark them "A BRIEF Blessing."
- ❏ Set a collection goal. Give weekly progress reports.
- ❏ Begin or end with a special BRIEF Blessing Sunday.
- ❏ Invite an agency representative to be present to help kick off the campaign.
- ❏ Enlist enough drivers to transport the group to discount stores to purchase underwear.
- ❏ Provide permission slips to the tweens and make sure to get them signed by parents and guardians.

GATHER 'N' GAB (20–45 minutes)

As the tweens arrive, ask them to:

- ❏ Make signs for the cardboard boxes.
- ❏ Wrap the boxes as Christmas gifts, leaving the top open.
- ❏ Place the boxes throughout the church.

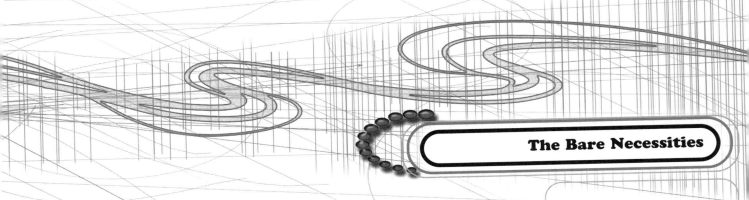

GOD'S WORD (15–20 minutes)

Have one of the tweens read aloud **Matthew 25:31-40** (when you do kindness to others, you do it to Christ Jesus).

Invite the tweens in pairs to act out both the positive and negative responses. Afterward, ask them what insights they gained and what they think is the meaning of the Scripture.

If need be, speak briefly about this Bible passage, using the following information:

In the context of the judgment parables of Chapter 25, Jesus talks about dividing the sheep from the goats. The "sheep" represent those who—

- when I was hungry, gave me something to eat,
- when I was thirsty, gave me something to drink,
- when I was a stranger, invited me in,
- when I was naked, clothed me,
- when I was sick, looked after me, and
- when I was in prison, visited me.

In contrast, the "goats" are those who failed to do these things. As he concludes this analogy, Jesus says:

"Truly I tell you, just as you did it to one of the least of these who are members of my family, you did it to me" (**Matthew 25:40**).

Ask specifically what Jesus' words mean for us today.

Say: **In persons who are hungry or thirsty, strangers, and even prisoners, Jesus is waiting for our touch of love. If you're wondering what God looks like today, look into the eyes of the hungry people in your community, the homeless in the inner city, the people in prisons, the strangers at your school, and the poor who don't even have enough money to buy underwear. God is waiting to meet you through them.**

Pray: **Dear God, as we collect undergarments for needy families, may we remember that we are doing this for and to you. You are waiting to receive these gifts of love. Bless this special outreach program we pray. Amen.**

Special Tips

- ❑ Redundant publicity will be your best friend. Publicize, publicize, publicize! Publicize in the bulletin and newsletter, from the pulpit, on posters, by word of mouth, and so on.
- ❑ Some rental truck locations will sell boxes at a reduced rate for projects like this. It doesn't hurt to ask.
- ❑ Check with your local grocery or appliance stores. They will often provide various sizes of boxes free of charge.
- ❑ Be careful when selecting a co-sponsor. Do your research! Clarify expectations. Many will serve as your underwear distributor, but nothing else.
- ❑ Some businesses and schools may want to participate too.

The Bare Necessities

Helpful Tips

- ❑ Let the tweens do the math. Don't do it for them.
- ❑ Remind the tweens about sales tax!
- ❑ They can use only the money they brought ($5 each), but they can work together to make purchases.
- ❑ You can add $5 to the total, but that's all.
- ❑ Remind them to look for specials.
- ❑ Tell the tweens to purchase underwear in a variety of sizes.
- ❑ Tweens are not allowed to ask shoppers for money.
- ❑ Tell the tweens not to buy anything gaudy or risque.

TWEENS IN MISSION (60–90 minutes)

- ❑ Take the tweens, with their five dollars to a discount store. Be sure to count everyone before you leave and talk about proper behavior:
  - No running off by yourself
  - Stay with your group
  - Stick to the task at hand
  - Now is not the time to purchase personal items
- ❑ Set a "safe meeting place" should someone get separated from the group.
- ❑ Set a shopping time limit. Have them divide into smaller groups (one adult per group) and determine where to meet before getting into vehicles to return to the church.
- ❑ Give them the task of seeing how many pairs of adult (or children's) underwear you can purchase. (It's OK to work together.)
- ❑ Once all of the purchases are made, return to the church. Be sure to count everyone before you leave. You don't want to leave anyone behind.

SNACK 'N' YACK (20–30 minutes)

Upon returning to the church, serve the snack. Afterward, ask:

- Did you have fun today?
- How many pairs of underwear did you purchase?
- Were you surprised by that number? Did you expect to purchase more? less?

As a group, place the underwear in the receptacles.

Say: **Agencies say that persons who are poor often cannot afford "luxury" items such as underwear. Can you believe that? Underwear garments are luxury items for some people. It's hard for us to imagine. Fortunately, our time of fun will be a "brief" blessing for them. And in serving the needs of others, we are showing our love to Jesus.**

SENDING FORTH (2–5 minutes)

Pray: **O God, as we work on this special collection drive, please bless and multiply our efforts. May others know of our love because of this "brief" blessing. Amen.**

7 Care Packages

LESSON IN A NUTSHELL:

The apostle Paul often took time to remember and pray for faraway friends. Friends he had made in his journeys had not escaped his memory; Paul remembered and prayed for them. In this lesson your tweens will remember and pray for students going away to college. By preparing care packages for first-year college students, tweens can show others that they have not been forgotten.

DISCOVERING THE NEED

Everyone loves to receive packages in the mail, especially youth leaving the security of home and church for the first time. Therefore, why not remember college freshmen by sending them college care packages?

To get started, you will need the college mailing addresses of your church's freshmen. The church office is a good place to begin gathering up-to-date addresses. Parents of the students may be your best source.

Something to Consider

One church began sending care packages to their college freshmen several years ago. Both the parents and freshmen were amazed by (and grateful for) this act of love. Because of the project's popularity and impact, care packages are now included in the church's annual budget (under young adult ministry).

The larger care packages (about $50 is spent on each one) are sent to freshmen (including a nice study Bible). Smaller care packets (containing just a letter and computer discs or highlighters, for example) are mailed to all of the remaining college students. Now that sending the care packages has become an annual tradition, all of the college students eagerly await them.

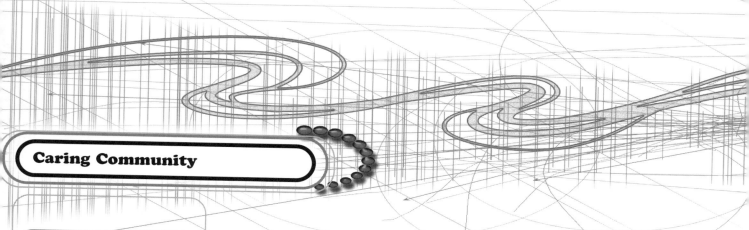

Caring Community

What You Will Need

- ☐ Large mailing envelopes or small to medium cardboard boxes (depending on the number and size of the items collected)
- ☐ Enough "thinking of you" cards for each freshman (handmade, computer-generated or boxed cards will do fine)
- ☐ Markers and pencils
- ☐ Tables for the supplies
- ☐ Collected items
- ☐ Purchased items
- ☐ Tape to seal the boxes

GET READY

- ☐ Contact the parents of the freshmen to see whether they would like to include any personal items in the boxes.
- ☐ Place a wish list in the church newsletter (see the list below).
- ☐ Contact the students' former Sunday school class or small group to see whether they would like to send anything.
- ☐ Ask if your youth or children's ministry budget can cover all or a portion of this project.
- ☐ Set a reasonable deadline for donated items to be submitted.
- ☐ Approach prospective donors or adult classes to see whether they would like to underwrite the expenses of this project.
- ☐ Be aware of possible expenses: cardboard boxes, items for the packages, wrapping and shipping supplies, postage, and postal insurance.
- ☐ Purchase or ask the tweens to bring items for the boxes.

GATHER 'N' GAB (15–30 minutes)

As the tweens arrive, have them help set-up the tables and supplies (an assembly line approach is recommended). Once the tables are set up, ask the tweens to sign "thinking of you" cards for each of the college students. Some may want to write short notes or letters.

GOD'S WORD (10–15 minutes)

Ask:

- Have you ever moved into a new neighborhood?
- How long ago did this happen?
- How did you feel?
- What (or whom) did you miss most?
- What was it like to be away from your friends?
- What was it like to leave your old church? your old school?
- How does it feel when your "old friends" write or call or visit you?
- Do you like being remembered by them?

Invite volunteers to read aloud these verses of thanksgiving and prayer for another: **Romans 1:8-10; Ephesians 1:16; Philippians 1:3; 2 Timothy 1:3; Philemon 1:4.**

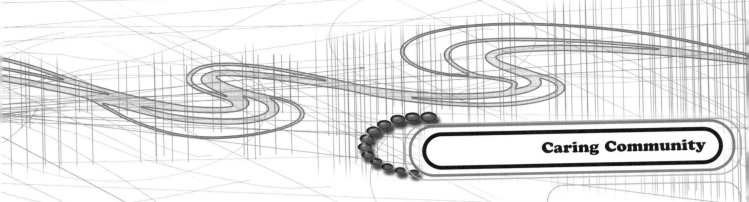

Ask:

- What do all of these verses have in common?
- What key words were repeated? (*remember* and *prayer*)

Say: **Although the writer of these verses could no longer be close to his friends, he continually remembered and prayed for them from a distance.**

Ask:

- If you moved away, would you like to be remembered?
- How would it feel to know that "old" friends were remembering and praying for you?
- Now that our college students have gone (or are going) away to college, how do you think they feel? Do you think that they would enjoy being remembered? Do you think that they would enjoy knowing that we had prayed for them?

Tell the tweens that today they will have a chance to do both.

TWEENS IN MISSION (20–45 minutes)

Preparing the care packages

❏ Be an observer and guide as the tweens prepare the care packages themselves.
❏ Gently guide them to divide the supplies equally.
❏ Make sure any specialty or personal items go in the correct boxes.
❏ Ask one of them (with good handwriting) to address the outside of the boxes. (You may need to provide some guidance.) A fine-tip permanent marker is recommended.
❏ Seal the boxes later. (It will give you a chance to add your personal letter.)
❏ Write (and include) a personal letter that says something like: "Just wanted you to know our tweens prepared this gift for you. They hope that you enjoy it! When we finished this special project, we prayed for you. We thought that you might like to know that. We're thinking about you. God bless you!"

Special Tips

❏ Ask for donors. You'll be surprised by the number of people (and groups) who are willing to provide financial assistance or items.
❏ The church might already have budgeted money available for this project. Check it out.
❏ Items can be donated, purchased in bulk, or a combination of the two.
❏ Avoid items that can melt, leak, or break easily.
❏ When you deliver the sealed boxes to your local post office for weighing and proper postage, it's smart to insure them.
❏ For optimum effect, mail the packages shortly after school starts or close to final exams.
❏ Ask the church secretary to add "college students away" to the church mailing list and to the church prayer list. Make sure that their college address is added to the church's general mailing list too!

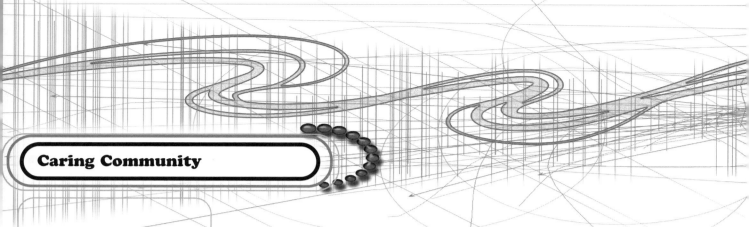

SNACK 'N' YACK (30 minutes)

As the tweens finish their snack, ask:

- What did you like most about this project?
- Did you enjoy "remembering" our college students?
- When they open their packages, how do you think they will feel?
- Is there anything else you would like to do for them (at a later date)?
- In our Scripture passages, two words were repeated several times. What were they?
- So far, we've remembered our college students by preparing care packages, now it's time to pray for them too.

SENDING FORTH (5–10 minutes)

Choose a prayer option that is best suited for you and your group:

Option 1: Ask the group to make a circle around the boxes, holding hands. Lead the group in a prayer. If you prefer, you can start a popcorn prayer, ask for tween volunteers to pray, or pray yourself.

Option 2: Ask your tweens to place their hands on a specific box, and pray for that freshman by name. Do the same for each of the remaining boxes.

If you are leading a group prayer, you could say: **God, please bless all of the young adults represented by these care packages. May your Spirit guide them, may these gifts bring a smile to their faces, and may your love comfort them while they are away. Amen.**

If you are leading a prayer for a specific student, you could say: **God, please bless our friend _____. May your Spirit guide (her or him), may this gift bring a smile to (her or his) face, and may your love comfort (her or him) while (she or he) is away. Amen.**

Special Tips (Continued)

- ❑ Before the tweens arrive, you may want to set up the boxes and supplies in an assembly line. Some groups prefer to make set-up a part of the activity.
- ❑ Try to make all of the packages the same or nearly the same. Close friends and students attending the same college will compare packages.
- ❑ Send care packages to all college freshmen—commuters and dorm students.
- ❑ Students attending trade schools, joining the military, or joining the work force should receive a package too. The content of these packages should be tailor-made for each person, if possible.
- ❑ If you can afford to send packages to all of your college students (not just the freshmen), then do it. College students love mail from home!

8 Food for the Hungry

LESSON IN A NUTSHELL

The tweens will learn through Bible study and hands-on service about God's call to feed the hungry. The tweens will collect and deliver food as well as provide direct service to a hunger-related agency.

DISCOVERING THE NEED

Jesus said, "Feed my sheep" (**John 21:15-17**). Who are the people in your community who are hungry? Locate hunger-related agencies in your community. Is there a church food bank or soup kitchen nearby? Check with other churches in your area to see what they are doing for the hungry? Find an agency such as a food bank, Meals on Wheels, or a soup kitchen where the tweens can be in direct, hands-on service.

Something to Consider

After visiting a local soup kitchen, a tween in Arkansas passed a man on the highway with a sign that read, "Will work for food." She and her family discussed the probability that this man was unaware of the local soup kitchen.

Her family designed and made maps giving directions to the soup kitchen and the phone number to call for information. These maps were placed at bus stations, hospital emergency rooms, and the local police station.

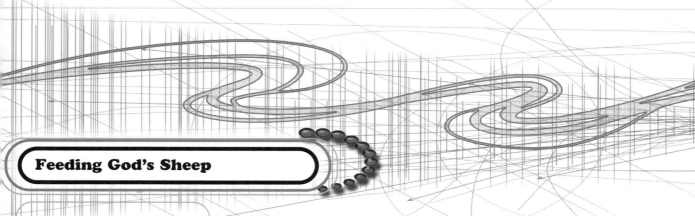

Feeding God's Sheep

What You Will Need

❑ Small brown paper bags (one per tween)
❑ Chocolate candy, hard candy, oat cereal such as Cheerios®
❑ Old magazines, scissors, glue, newsprint
❑ Paper sacks to carry food donations, any items need to complete your service such as food service gloves. Check with your chosen agency for details.

Prepare the Bags

Each Tween will fill one bag. Fill the bags as indicated:

❑ 1 of every 6 bags contains 8 pieces of chocolate candy.
❑ 2 of every 6 bags contains 3 pieces of hard candy.
❑ 3 of every 6 bags contains 7 cups of dry cereal.

GET READY

❑ One month prior to the meeting, contact a local food bank, Meals on Wheels, or a soup kitchen to arrange your visit and service project.
❑ Be sure to have signed transportation permission forms.
❑ One week prior to your meeting, send a note to the tweens, reminding them to bring canned or dry food for your chosen mission.
❑ Call the agency one or two days before to confirm your visit.
❑ Fill the bags for the Gather 'n' Gab activity, as indicated below.
❑ Set out magazines, scissors, glue, and newsprint for a food collage.

GATHER 'N' GAB (10–15 minutes)

As the tweens arrive, randomly distribute the bags, instructing the tweens not to open them until everyone has arrived.

Say: **This is your snack for today. Please do not open your bag until instructed to do so. Take a few minutes to add to our food collage.**

Instruct the tweens to find pictures of their favorite foods, people who are hungry, people who are satisfied, and so on.

When all of the tweens have arrived, invite them to sit in a circle and enjoy their snack. There is to be no sharing of snacks, and they are to attempt to eat all that is in their bag. (Be sensitive to food allergies.) Encourage the tweens to try to eat everything in their bags.

When the tweens have eaten their snack, gather the them into small groups, with an adult or older youth leader. Use these or similar questions to lead a discussion of the snack experience.

- What was your first thought when you opened your snack bag?
- How did you feel watching the others eat their snacks?
- What actions did you want to take?

In addition, you may want to use the activity "World Hunger" in the box on the next page to reinforce the learnings here.

Direct the tweens' attention to their collage. Ask:

- What does our collage tell others about our understanding of food?
- What does our collage tell others about God?

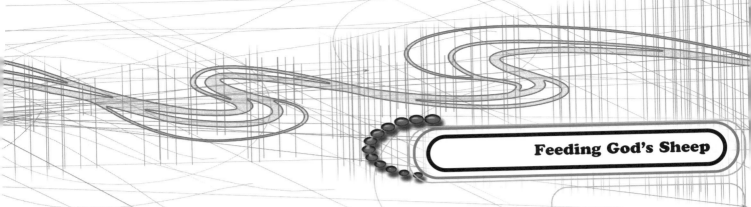

GOD'S WORD (10–15 minutes)

Have volunteers read aloud the following Scripture lessons:

Proverbs 22:9 (Generous people are blessed for sharing with the poor.)
John 21:15-19 (Feed my sheep.)

Lead the tweens in a discussion of the Scripture, using the information below.

Both the Old and New Testaments indicate that God desires that we share what we have with others. The Proverb text indicates that blessings will come to those who share. According to the John text, those who love Jesus will feed the hungry.

Note that Jesus repeats the question to Peter three times. In the Bible, the number three is a sign of completeness. For Jesus, this command is complete and absolute. The repetition of the question indicates the importance of the response. If we truly love Jesus, we will follow Jesus' commands and will care for those who are hungry.

Pray: **Dear God, help us care for those who are less fortunate than we are. Help us love you by feeding and caring for others. Help us be blessed by our service to you. Amen.**

TWEENS IN MISSION (1–2 hours)

Prepare your tweens for the trip by explaining where you are going and what you will be doing as an act of service. Help the tweens fill the sacks with food donations to take.

Be sure to have made prior arrangements with a specific agency or mission. Gather information for your chosen agency to share with the tweens before your visit. Some hands-on service options are:

Meals on Wheels: Visit the local Meals on Wheels agency. Activities could include helping prepare food, cleaning the food preparation area, assisting in distribution to the drivers, or actual delivery of the meals.

Food Bank: Visit the local food bank or distribution center. Activities could include sorting of food donations, stocking shelves, preparing a bulk mailing, or assisting with food distribution.

Soup Kitchen: Visit a local soup kitchen or hot meal mission. Activities could include food preparation, serving, or cleaning.

World Hunger

❑ Line up six tweens to represent the world. Pull aside one to represent the high-income people and nations (17%). In this group, most people make enough money to live comfortably, most children have safe water and good doctors, many people get more to eat than they need.

❑ Pull out one and a half youth (that will be fun!). These represent nations and people in the middle range (25%). These people don't get enough to eat, and five times more children die in this group than in the first group.

❑ Indicate the remaining three and a half tweens. They represent the more than half the world (57%) who earn less than $2 a day. Most of these people go hungry every day. The drinking water often makes them sick, and some even die from drinking it.

Bread for the World (**www.bread.org**)

One in Ten

According to Bread for the World, 33 million people—including 13 million children—in the United States alone live in households that experience hunger or the uncertainty of where the next meal is coming from. This represents one in ten households (10 percent).

For more information and additional ways to engage youth in hunger-related ministry and social action, go to the Bread for the World website: *www.bread.org.*

SNACK 'N' YACK (15–20 minutes)

If possible, hold the response time at the chosen service site.

Gather the tweens into small groups. Lead the tweens in a discussion of their experience in serving the hungry. Ask open-ended questions that relate to your particular experience. Ask questions regarding particular people. Use the following or similar questions in your discussion:

- What did it feel like to _____? (clean the kitchen, stock shelves, serve soup)
- What was your first thought when _____? (the people came in to eat)
- How were you blessed by today's act of service?
- Are there ways we can continue to be in service in this place?

SENDING FORTH (2–5 minutes)

Say: **Today we learned more about what it means to be hungry. We also learned what is expected of those who say they love God.**

Before we close in prayer, you may share your concerns for yourself, your family, or others so that they may be lifted to God in prayer.

Invite the tweens to write down prayer requests so that they may be included in the closing prayer. Ask one of the tweens to lead the following closing prayer:

Pray: **Dear God, thank you for loving us enough to send your son, Jesus, to show us how to love and care for others. Help us be willing to give of ourselves to help others. Today we lift up these concerns and praises: (*read the written requests*). Thank you for blessing us through our mission. Amen.**

9 Clean Generosity

LESSON IN A NUTSHELL

Your tweens will "open their hands" to the needy by delivering free newspapers, magazines, fabric softener sheets, and laundry detergent to laundromats throughout your community.

DISCOVERING THE NEED

Oftentimes persons who use laundromats are persons who need to make every penny count. Supplying necessities such as detergent and luxuries such as magazines, newspapers, and fabric softener is one way of showing Christ's love.

You will need to locate laundromats in your community, particularly those in needy neighborhoods. The telephone book and Internet are good resources for this information.

Something to Consider

One church divided into three groups and visited eight laundromats in one evening. Although surprised, the patrons expressed an overwhelming appreciation for the thoughtful gifts.

Interestingly, the ones most amazed were the laundromat attendants. One said, "I have overseen laundromats most of my adult life, and this is the first time a church has ever shown any interest in us."

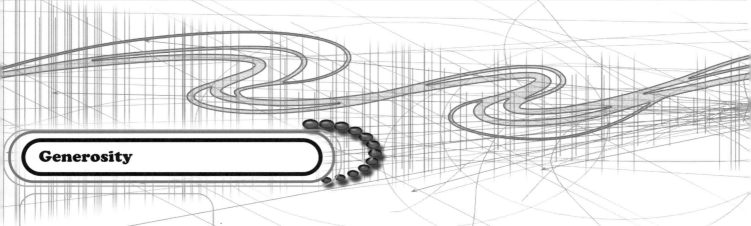

Generosity

What You Will Need

- ❏ Laundry detergent tabs or small boxes (Don't forget gentle detergent for baby clothes.)
- ❏ Fabric softener sheets
- ❏ Zip-type plastic bags (sandwich size)
- ❏ Copies of your local newspaper
- ❏ New (or gently used) magazines
- ❏ Maps for each driver (include address and phone number of each site)
- ❏ Laundromat cards (see the margin on page 82)

GET READY

- ❏ Locate all of the laundromats you would like to visit. Each group should have enough time to visit 2–4 locations (each).
- ❏ Call the laundromat attendants (or owners) to tell them about the project.
- ❏ Enlist adult drivers. (Don't forget permission slips!)
- ❏ Some laundromats have an attendant; others do not. It is advisable to visit each attendant (calling is your second best choice) to introduce yourself, to describe the project, and to address concerns and questions.
- ❏ Be prepared to be greeted with skepticism. Many will wonder whether any strings are attached—handing out religious tracts, fundraising, and so forth. Your pre-trip visit or phone call will allow you to address their questions and concerns.
- ❏ Don't be surprised if some will not allow you to visit. Thank them for their time, and move on to the next location on your list.

GATHER 'N' GAB (15–20 minutes)

As the tweens arrive, ask them to:

- ❏ Place four or five fabric softener sheets in each plastic bag.
- ❏ Separate the magazines, newspapers, detergent tabs, and softener baggies into routes. Every route will need a stack of each item.
- ❏ Make laundromat cards, as needed (see the margin on page 82).
- ❏ Divide the tweens into teams of four or five, plus an adult driver.

GOD'S WORD (15–20 minutes)

Have volunteers read aloud the following Scriptures:

Deuteronomy 15:7-8, 10-11 (Generously give to the needy.)
2 Corinthians 8:1-15 (Paul commends the example of the Macedonians' generosity to the Christians in Corinth.)

Ask:

- The Macedonian church had more than enough problems of their own—one of them being poverty. Why do you suppose they wanted to help the Jerusalem church? (*They felt compassion for the needy; they wanted to do their part.*)
- Why did Moses command the children of Israel to help the poor? (*Both the giver and receiver are blessed; if you don't help, who will?*)

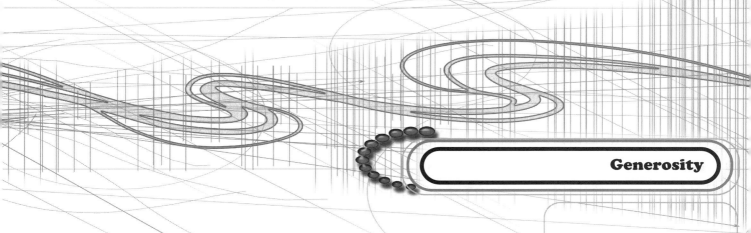

- Why should we help others? Won't someone else take care of the needy? (*It's our responsibility to do what we can; we shouldn't overlook needs.*)
- Why should we take free detergent, magazines and newspapers, and fabric sheets to local laundromats? (*To do what we can to help, to demonstrate God's love for others, to be faithful in following Moses' command, to follow the example of the Macedonians*)
- Besides helping people at the laundromats, what could our group do sometime later to help the poor or hungry? What could your family do? What could you do?

Invite other questions and comments about the verses.

Pray: **Dear God, place upon our hearts those whom you would have us care for so that we might experience the grace of giving and so that others might experience the grace of receiving. Bless us that we might be a blessing to others today. Amen.**

TWEENS IN MISSION (60–90 minutes)

- ❑ Divide the group into smaller teams.
- ❑ Have each group choose a spokesperson, preferably one of the tweens.
- ❑ Provide each group with a map (if needed) and the address and phone number of the laundromats.
- ❑ Provide the name of the contact person.
- ❑ Leave extra laundromat cards, detergent and fabric sheets, newspapers, and magazines in the waiting area. Although some of the patrons may not accept your gift when you are present, they may take them after you leave.
- ❑ Give a time limit (usually around 60 minutes) and meet back at the church for debriefing and snacks.
- ❑ Encourage everyone to be friendly and to be on their best behavior.
- ❑ Give each team member a separate responsibility. One can be the spokesperson, another can distribute the cards, a third can hand out magazines, and so forth.
- ❑ Tell the tweens to keep this in mind: Don't be offended if someone refuses your gift. Simply say, "God bless you!" and move on to the next person.
- ❑ Some of the patrons may be distant or skeptical. Be prepared to explain what you're doing. Give each patron a laundromat card (and a set of items) and say, "This is a free gift from our tweens—no strings attached!"
- ❑ Some of the patrons may want to talk for awhile. Listen attentively to their questions, comments, and stories; and stay as long as needed. The

Special Tips

Use detergent tabs, not liquid or powder. They're easier to handle.

Provide current newspapers, not old ones.

Take recent magazines; less than six months old.

Don't "gang up" on the patrons. Taking 11–14 tweens in a van is not advisable. Besides overwhelming the patrons, several of your tweens will be left with nothing to do. It's more effective to travel in smaller groups.

Decide how many newspapers, magazines, detergent tabs, and fabric softener bags will be needed. The amount will vary depending on the size and number of laundromats. It's better to take too much, rather than not enough.

Consider placing a collection list in the church newsletter to help defray expenses, and to allow a larger number of people to participate.

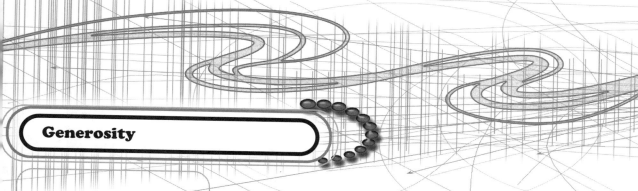

Laundromat Cards

Laundromat cards can be created in different formats. The smaller, business card size seems to work best.

If you prefer, the message can be computer-generated (or hand printed) on sticky mailing labels and affixed to each plastic bag. Or they may be prepared as a folded greeting card with the message inside.

Larger half-page or full-page formats are not recommended. They will become a litter problem for the laundromat (and you).

Your cards should say something such as:

"This gift of love was provided by the fifth and sixth graders of XYZ church."

Keep the message short, and create enough cards for each patron.

relationships you make and the stories you hear will be remembered for a long time! Take time to savor the full experience!

❑ Remind the tweens not to stare or point and to be polite. Have them practice before you leave what they might say and do.

❑ Regardless of their apparent need, offer the free gifts to every patron. Don't leave anyone out.

❑ If there are no patrons in the laundromat, leave laundromat cards, detergent, magazines, and newspapers in the waiting area. They will be put to good use later.

❑ Don't forget to smile.

SNACK 'N' YACK (15–30 minutes)

Upon returning to the church, serve light refreshments and ask for volunteers from each team to describe the laundromats and the people they met. Give each group a chance to respond. Hearing all of the reports is very important.

Ask:

- How did people respond to your help?
- How did today's experience make you feel?
- Did you enjoy helping other people? Would you enjoy doing it again?
- If you could help somewhere else, where would you want to go? Why?

SENDING FORTH (2–5 minutes)

Pray: **In the power of the Holy Spirit, send us forth, O God, to care for persons who are poor, persons who are hungry—for our neighbors in need. May the love of God rest upon us now and upon those we serve. Amen.**

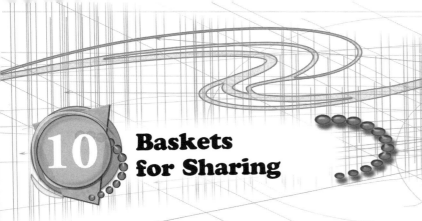

10 Baskets for Sharing

LESSON IN A NUTSHELL

The tweens will discuss kindness, ways to express kindness, and the biblical basis for acts of kindness. They will make gift baskets to be filled with various items appropriate to the chosen recipients.

DISCOVERING THE NEED

Most everyone enjoys the delight of getting an unexpected gift. Who are the people nearby who rarely have that joy? Look at your church membership and attendance rolls for persons who are homebound or ill. Is there a hospital, nursing home, or senior citizens center within easy driving distance? What other agencies in your community might welcome such gifts for the people they serve?

Something to Consider

The Froggers Fellowship group at Sierra Vista United Methodist Church, in San Angelo, Texas, makes "Baskets for Sharing" each spring. The pastors deliver these baskets as they make regular home and hospital visits throughout the year.

One spring the Froggers received this message from someone who had received a basket: "Thank you for the lovely basket. Sometimes I feel so alone and cut off from my church family. Your gift reminds me that I am not alone."

The pastors report that the baskets are being used to hold mail, craft supplies, and other items. These baskets help the senior adults feel that they are a part of the community of Christ.

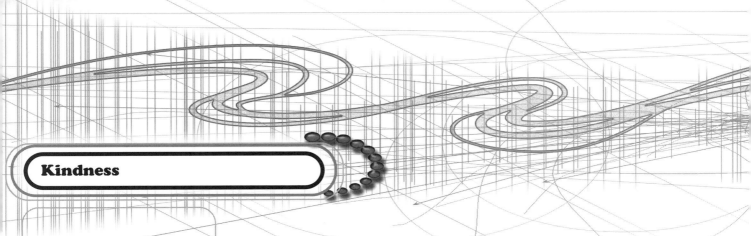

Kindness

What You Will Need

- Paper
- Pencils
- Tape
- Lunch size paper sacks (2 per basket)
- Card stock, fancy and regular scissors, paper punch, thin ribbon or yarn
- Untwisted paper twist or wide fabric ribbon
- Easter grass or shredded gift wrap paper
- Extra supplies to make a basket for the group to use as their own prayer basket

Suggested items for bags

- Small snack crackers or food packs
- Small packages of mints
- Tea or coffee singles
- Small packages of tissues
- Note cards and postage stamps
- Fresh flowers
- Small toys

GET READY

- One month prior to the meeting, arrange to deliver the gift baskets to home-bound members of your church, a homeless shelter, nursing home, or similar agency. If you cannot arrange a direct visit, ask to give the bags to your pastor to deliver during pastoral calls.
- One week prior to the meeting, send a note to the tween, instructing them to bring small items to put into the gift baskets. (See the suggestions at left.) These items will vary, depending upon the planned recipients.
- If your group is going to deliver the bags, be sure to make arrangements for delivery of the bags. Have travel permission forms for each tween.
- Call ahead to reconfirm your appointments.
- Make a sample gift basket. This basket can be used as the class prayer basket.
- Print Gather 'n' Gab scenarios on large paper and place a sign that says, "What do you think?" next to the paper.

GATHER 'N' GAB (10–15 minutes)

Scenario 1: John has just moved to town. His neighbor arrives with a freshly made chocolate cake to welcome John's family to the neighborhood. As the neighbor is leaving, John says, "I don't like chocolate cake."

Scenario 2: Sharon received two of the same game for her birthday. She sent thank-you notes to both people. Sharon decided to give the extra game to Maggie, a girl down the street. Sharon and Maggie became good friends.

Scenario 3: Mr. Jones lives all alone. Suzy and Liam offered to mow his yard for him. Mr. Jones refused to let them mow it for free. He insisted on paying them. Suzy and Liam did not want to be paid; they were trying to be friendly.

Gather the tweens into small groups, with an adult or older youth leader. Invite the tweens to talk about their responses to the scenarios and the following questions:

- How would you define *kindness*?
- What different ways have you responded to kindness?
- Have you ever been put down because of your kindness?
- Has anyone ever rejected your act of kindness?

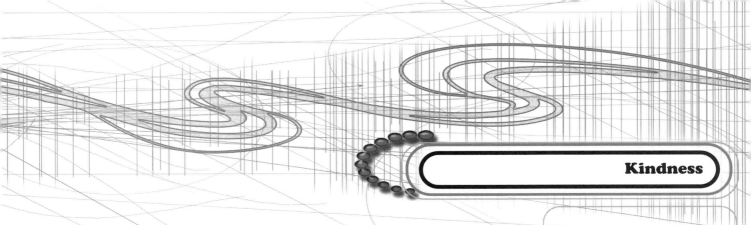

GOD'S WORD (10–15 minutes)

Have one of the tweens read aloud **Micah 6:8** (The Lord requires kindness).

Lead the tweens in a discussion of the Scripture, using the information below.

Say: **The Book of Micah is found in the Old Testament. Also in the New Testament are many stories in which Jesus explains how to do justice, love kindness, and walk humbly with God. The parable of the Good Samaritan is an excellent example of an act of kindness.**

Invite one of the tweens to read the story of the Good Samaritan from **Luke 10:25-37.** With this parable, Jesus changes the notions about who is a neighbor. According to Jesus, a neighbor is one who displays kindness to another. The Levite and the priest were most likely concerned about getting on with their duties. They did not take time to stop to help. The Samaritan, even though a foreigner in that land, took the time to stop and help.

Pray: **Dear God, we seek ways to share your love with others. Help us see ways to be kind to people we know and to people we do not know. And all God's children said: Amen.**

TWEENS IN MISSION (1–2 hours)

Tell the tweens that they will be making gift baskets for people who are sometimes forgotten by society. Ask the tweens to name some categories of people who are sometimes forgotten by society? (*older adults, people with cancer, children without parents, and so on*) Tell the tweens about the group of persons they will be serving today; remind them that their thoughtfulness will help those persons know that God loves them.

Follow the steps in Making the Baskets (right) and Special Tips (in the margin on page 86) to construct the baskets. When the baskets are complete, add a small amount of gift-wrap shreds or Easter grass and fill it with gift items.

Attach a gift tag made of cardstock or construction paper. Use fancy-edge scissors to cut out the tag. Have the tweens write a short note on the gift tag, and tell them to be sure to sign their name.

If you have time, deliver the gift baskets to shut-ins, a nursing home, a hospital, or other similar agency or group of people. If you cannot arrange a visit, give the gift baskets to the pastor to deliver when he or she makes pastoral care calls in homes or hospitals.

Making the Baskets

❏ Insert one open lunch bag inside another for strength. Fold over the tops to the inside so that they touch the bottom.

❏ Cut lengths of ribbon about 20 inches long Wrap the ribbon down one side of the bag, across the bottom, and up the other side. Fold the ends of the ribbon over the rim of the bag and glue them to the inside of the rim. Repeat the process, using more lengths of ribbon, placing each successive ribbon next the the previous one. Cover all four sides of the bag in the same manner. (It is OK if part of the bag shows through.)

❏ Measure the circumference of the bag, cutting strips of ribbon 2 inches longer. Weave this ribbon in and out around the bag, gluing the ends together.

❏ Braid three 18-inch strips of ribbon together for the handle, and staple the ends of the handle to the sides of the bag.

85

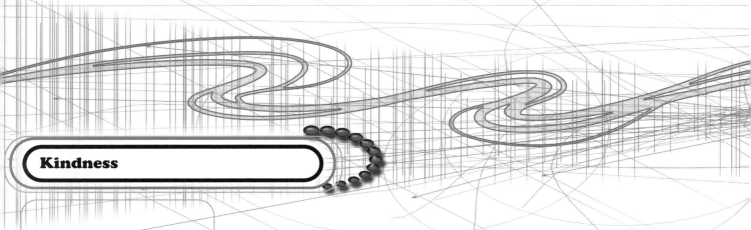

Special Tips

You might want to set up an assembly line to make the bags. Try this:

❑ Bag preparers put the two bags together.
❑ Bag folders fold the sides down.
❑ Cutters cut the ribbon to the correct length. (Be sure to measure first.)
❑ Gluers glue the ribbons around the bags. (This step might require more persons than the previous steps do.)
❑ Weavers weave ribbons around the bags. (Since weaving takes longer than the other steps, have additional weavers.)
❑ Braiders braid the handles.
❑ Staplers staple on the handles.
❑ Fillers fill the baskets with goodies.
❑ Writers write the tag information.
❑ Taggers attach the tags to the bags.

Be sure to notice where on the assembly line more or fewer helpers are needed.

SNACK 'N' YACK (15–20 minutes)

Gather the tweens into groups of 4 or 5 to discuss the experience of delivering the gift baskets. Talk about the people they visited and the response of these people to the gifts. Use the following or similar questions in your discussion:

▪ What one thing will you remember about delivering or making these baskets?
▪ What was the hardest thing about delivering or making these baskets?
▪ How did the people we delivered the baskets to respond?
▪ What was the most inspiring thing about delivering these baskets?
▪ Were any of the people negative about our visit?
▪ Can you think of other ways we can care for any of these people?
▪ What does our project have to do with today's Scripture lesson?

SENDING FORTH (2–5 minutes)

Say: **Today we experienced an act of caring for others. By showing our concern for others, we share God's love with them.**

Before the closing prayer, encourage the tweens to write on paper slips their prayer concerns for themselves, their families, and others. Then have the tweens place the slips in the group prayer basket. Invite one of the tweens to lead the closing prayer.

Pray: **Dear God, thank you for our time together today. We have learned that sometimes we forget to show your love to others. Help us be more loving and kind to others and be thankful when others are kind to us. We lift up the following individuals and concerns to you today: (*read the prayer concerns from the basket*). Thank you for hearing and responding to our prayers. Amen.**

11 Hospitality Check

LESSON IN A NUTSHELL

The tweens will discover the biblical basis for hospitality. They will evaluate the hospitality level of their congregation and will tell church leadership their recommendations for improvement. They will make "Welcome Visitor" bookmarks or "Ask Me About" buttons as a way of welcoming newcomers.

DISCOVERING THE NEED

Coming into a new place is intimidating for many people. Will they be noticed? Will they be welcomed? Will they fit in? are questions that visitors bring with them to church. A warm and welcoming experience makes a difference in how new persons feel about the church and in their decision to continue to grow spiritually with this community of faith. How are visitors welcomed to your church?

Something to Consider

Who in your congregation is always the first person to be at the hospital when someone is sick or to take food to someone's house? Invite that person to come to your tweens group to talk about hospitality.

Who in your congregation is always smiling, inviting people to attend church, or standing at the front door? Invite that person to come to your tweens group to share his or her ideas about welcoming others into the life of the church.

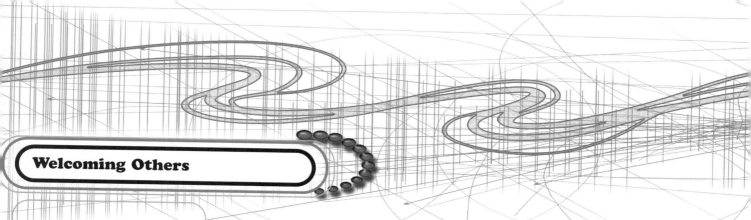

Welcoming Others

What You Will Need

- ❑ Photocopies of instructions on page 91 or index cards
- ❑ Signs on construction paper: Welcome, Keep Out, Members Only, Open to Everyone, No Shirt—No Shoes—No Service, and others your tweens would recognize
- ❑ Information on your church's welcoming procedures
- ❑ "Hospitality Checklist" (page 92) and pencil for each tween
- ❑ Bookmark blanks (card stock or construction paper cut to 8½-by-2 strips)
- ❑ Markers
- ❑ Stickers
- ❑ Button blanks (card stock circles traced and cut from canning jar lid templates)
- ❑ Tape and safety pins

GET READY

- ❑ Gather information regarding the ways your church welcomes visitors.
- ❑ Talk with your pastor or worship committee, regarding options 2 and 3 in the Tweens in Mission section.
- ❑ Prepare a copy of the "Hospitality Checklist" (page 92) for each tween.
- ❑ Make signs for the Gather 'n' Gab activity.
- ❑ Gather supplies for bookmarks and buttons.
- ❑ Photocopy the instructions on page 91. Cut them apart and give them to individuals as they arrive. (Or write the instructions on index cards to give to the tweens.)

GATHER 'N' GAB (10–15 minutes)

As you give the tweens their instructions, tell them to follow the directions on the card until all have arrived.

Afterward, gather to talk about the experience. If your group is large, divide the tweens into smaller groups of four or five, with an adult or older youth leader. Lead the tweens in a discussion using these or similar questions:

- How did people respond to you?
- Did you feel welcomed? By which person?
- How did you feel about your actions?
- Have you ever gone someplace where you felt unwelcomed?
- What actions on the part of the people there made you feel unwelcome?
- How did you respond in that situation?

GOD'S WORD (10–15 minutes)

Have volunteers read aloud the following Scripture lessons:

Genesis 18:1-8 (Abraham shows hospitality to the three "men.")
Hebrews 13:1-2 (Do not neglect hospitality.)

Lead the tweens in a discussion of the Scripture, using the information below:

The Christian tradition of hospitality is rooted in the story of Abraham. He extended hospitality to the three "men" and later discovered that they were, indeed, God and two angels. Christians believe that Christ or God's messengers (angels) may come to us in the form of a strangers.

In Genesis, Abraham displayed hospitality to the three unknown visitors. Abraham gave the best of what he had to offer. Although the custom in that time and area of the world was to take the stranger into your home,

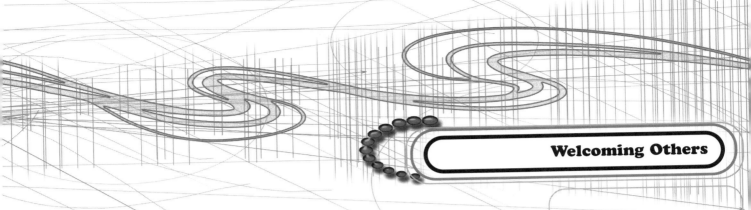

Abraham still had a choice about whether to do it and to what degree he would share from his own resources of food and shelter.

The Hebrews text reminds us that we who follow Christ cannot be choosy about to whom we will extend hospitality. Indeed, those who show God's love and care for people they do not even know may "entertain angels without knowing it."

Christian hospitality involves meeting the physical, social, and spiritual needs of people we don't already know or love. For Christians, hospitality is not so much a single action as it is a way of life that involves paying attention to the needs of people who are strangers to us.

In showing hospitality, we may also turn a stranger (a potential enemy) into a friend; at the very least, we affirm God's love for him or her. And sometimes, we encounter the risen Christ in unexpected ways through the stranger we welcome.

Pray. **Dear God, you welcome each of us into your loving care. By the example of Christ, we know the importance of hospitality, of welcoming strangers into your family. Help us show your hospitality to others. Amen.**

TWEENS IN MISSION (1–2 hours)

Ask:

- What do you think our church does to welcome visitors?

Write down the responses on large paper. Provide the tweens with information regarding the way your church welcomes visitors to the congregation and strangers who come for help. Lead the tweens in discussing what they think about how hospitable their congregation is.

Give each tween a "Hospitality Checklist" (page 92) and pencil. Ask the tweens whether they have anything to add to the list. Take the tweens on a tour of your church facilities, having them pay specific attention to the items on the checklist. If you have a large number of tweens, divide them into smaller groups and send them with an adult to different areas of your church complex. Set a designated return time.

When everyone had returned, discuss the tweens' findings. Talk about the following:

Special Tip

As you hear the stories of the tweens about how they have experienced being welcomed or excluded, consider taking a few minutes to roleplay ways of welcoming people.

Not all tweens have experience with such social skills. Allow them to practice so that they gain both know-how and confidence.

Reminder

Be sure to obtain permission from your pastor or worship committee for options 2 and 3.

- Ways we are a hospitable church
- Areas where we need improvement
- Ways we could make needed improvements

Then set up activities from these three options:

Option 1—Compose a letter or report to the administrative board or council, regarding the tweens' findings and recommendations.

Option 2—Make "Welcome Visitor" bookmarks, following instructions on page 91. These may be handed out in worship, mailed to visitors, or given to Sunday school teachers to hand out.

Option 3—Make "Ask Me About" buttons, following instructions on page 91 for greeters to wear on Sunday morning as they greet worshipers at the door. Invite the tweens to be Sunday morning greeters for a specified period of time.

SNACK 'N' YACK (15–20 minutes)

Gather the tweens into groups of four or five to discuss these questions:

- What were your feelings as you walked around our church?
- Were you surprised by your findings?
- What can you personally do to be more welcoming to others?
- What can others in the congregation do to be more welcoming?
- How welcome did you feel the first time you came to this group? Why?
- What can we do to welcome visitors to our group?
- Think of friends you could invite to join us. What would help them feel welcome?

SENDING FORTH (2–3 minutes)

Say: **Today we learned about being hospitable—caring for and welcoming others. By welcoming others into our community of faith, we are sharing God's love with them.**

Encourage the tweens to write down prayer requests to be included in the closing prayer. Invite one of the tweens to lead the closing prayer:

Pray: **Dear God, thank you for our time together today. We have learned the importance of welcoming others. We have learned of ways we can be more hospitable as a congregation. Help us to follow through with our plans for improvement. We lift up the following individuals and concerns to you today: (read the written requests). Thank you for listening to and responding to our prayers. Amen.**

Gather 'n' Gab Activity

When someone approaches you, roll your eyes, turn away, don't speak.

Greet everyone with a loud "howdy," shake his or her hand vigorously.

Walk around the room saying, "Where's the bathroom?"

Greet each person with a smile, say "Welcome to God's house," turn your back on him or her, and walk away.

When someone approaches you, lower your head, shuffle your feet, and mumble your name under your breath.

Walk up to each person and say, "May I help you?"

Bookmark Instructions

❑ Make 5–10 bookmarks by cutting 8½-by-11 sheets of card stock or construction paper into 8½-by-2 strips.
❑ Print "Welcome to Worship at (*insert the name of your church*)" on each bookmark.
❑ Decorate the bookmarks with stickers or drawings.

"Ask Me About" Buttons Instructions

❑ Use a canning jar lid as a pattern to trace onto card stock or posterboard to make a welcoming button.
❑ Write "Ask Me About (*insert the name of your church*)" on each button.
❑ Decorate the button with fun and friendly looking symbols, such as crosses, flowers, smiley faces.
❑ Glue or tape a safety pin to the back of each button.
❑ Make several buttons.
❑ Wear a button on Sunday mornings.

Hospitality Checklist

Name: _____   Date: _____

Our church is easy to locate.	___ Yes	___ No
Outdoor signs are visible are easy to read.	___ Yes	___ No
Indoor spaces are clearly marked.	___ Yes	___ No
The entrance to the church is clean and inviting.	___ Yes	___ No
The grass and outside areas are well maintained.	___ Yes	___ No
Buildings are clean and well maintained.	___ Yes	___ No
Greeters are ready to meet visitors.	___ Yes	___ No
Visitors are given information about the church.	___ Yes	___ No
Classes and groups are easy to locate.	___ Yes	___ No
The bulletin gives information about activities.	___ Yes	___ No
Visitors are personally welcomed by the pastor.	___ Yes	___ No
Follow-up phone calls are made to each visitor.	___ Yes	___ No
Classes and groups are notified of new visitors.	___ Yes	___ No
The congregation is friendly during/after services.	___ Yes	___ No
Visitor parking space is available close by.	___ Yes	___ No
Visitors receive a mailing or home-delivered gift.	___ Yes	___ No

12   Ministry Fair

LESSON IN A NUTSHELL

The tweens will review the various mission projects they have been involved in during the year. They will share their joys of fellowship and service by planning and presenting a "ministry fair" for the congregation.

DISCOVERING THE NEED

Many people in your congregation will be unaware of the needs of your community, the resources available to meet those needs, and the ways your tweens have been in ministry to your community. A ministry fair can inform your congregation and encourage them to greater support for the tweens and greater efforts for their own ministries.

The event can also serve to generate excitement for upcoming tweens for joining your fellowship group.

Something to Consider

For this lesson to be effective at the end of your year, you will need to begin planning early.

Allocate a short amount of time at the beginning of the year to discuss the "ministry fair" idea.

Plan to gather and save materials (including photographs) from each activity. Identify a place for safe keeping of the items.

Assign one or more tweens to be the group photographer(s). You may wish to carry a back-up camera yourself or buy a disposable camera for the group's use.

After each project ask one or two tweens to write a short synopsis of the activity while it is fresh on their minds.

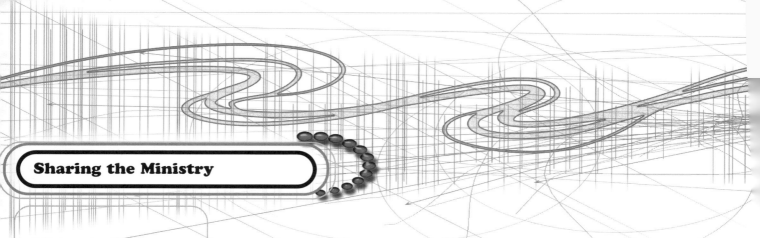

Sharing the Ministry

What You Will Need

- ❏ Posterboard
- ❏ Trifold display boards
- ❏ Glue
- ❏ Scissors
- ❏ Information from agencies
- ❏ Photos of your activities
- ❏ Samples of special gifts or items your group has made
- ❏ Supplies for making cookies or other refreshments for the fair
- ❏ Markers
- ❏ Large heart cutouts, one per tween and adult

GET READY

During the Year

- ❏ Plan ahead by gathering information and taking photographs of all your fellowship activities as you meet during the year.
- ❏ During each meeting, ask a volunteer to write a short summary of the mission activity and the response of the group to that activity.
- ❏ Set a date for the Ministry Fair and put it on the church calendar. The fair could be held in conjunction with a worship service—between, before, or after services. Or it could be related to a congregational fellowship meal.
- ❏ Gather brochures/booklets/information from each agency with which your group works.
- ❏ Save a sample of the items you make during the year.

As You Near the Event

- ❏ Publicize by putting invitations in bulletins and newsletters and having tween volunteers make announcements in worship.
- ❏ Send a special invitation to those who will be eligible to participate in your program next year.

GATHER 'N' GAB (10–15 minutes)

Post graffiti posters on the wall. On each poster, write the name of one activity from the year. As the tweens arrive, have them write their remembrances of each activity on the posters.

In small groups with an adult or older youth leader, lead the tweens in a discussion of the year's activities, using these or similar types of questions:

- Which service project did you like the best? Why?
- Which service project did you like the least? Why?
- Do you agree or disagree with the statements written on the graffiti posters?

GOD'S WORD (10–15 minutes)

Invite the tweens to choose and read aloud their favorite Scriptures from those used throughout the year. (You may need to have a list of the ones the group has studied.) Lead the tweens in a discussion, using these questions:

- Which of these Scriptures challenges you the most?
- Have you changed your attitude about any group or individual because of any of these Scriptures?

Invite the tweens to put several of the Scriptures in their own words.

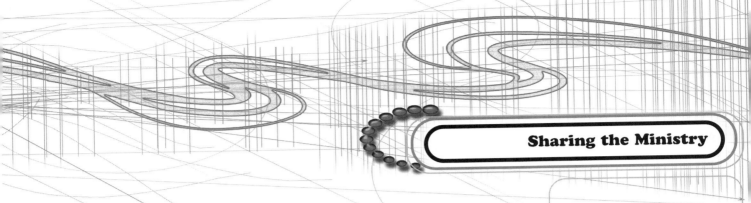

TWEENS IN MISSION (1-2 hours)

Divide the tweens into small groups to complete one or more of the following activities as preparation for the Ministry Fair:

Display Boards—Have several tweens construct display boards with photos and information about each of the year's activities. Be sure to have a separate board for each agency. Tweens may want to include a short section of the Scripture that related to the project.

Statements of Activity—Have some tweens compose a short synopsis of each activity. These may be attached to the display boards or used by a tween who will stand by each display board during the fair.

Invitations—Have tweens make posters inviting people to the Ministry Fair. These should be posted around the church at least two weeks prior to the fair. Have other tweens write bulletin and newsletter announcements. Have other tweens write invitations to the "rising" tweens who will be eligible to participate in the fellowship group the following year.

Program—Have some of the tweens develop a short skit that explains the purpose of the fellowship group. The skit could share some of the fun things that happened during the year.

Refreshments—Have several tweens make cookies or trail mix to serve as snacks during the Ministry Fair (and, perhaps, for snack today).

SNACK 'N' YACK (15-20 minutes)

Gather the tweens into small groups. Lead them in a discussion of the fun and Christian fellowship they have had during the past year. Be sure to recognize those who will be "graduating" from the tweens' fellowship and moving into the youth fellowship. Use these or similar questions:

- What will you remember most about your participation in this fellowship?
- What one thing would you like the group to remember about you?

Give the tweens each a large paper heart. Have them write their name in the middle of the heart. Gather the group into a circle and give each tween a pen. Pass the hearts around the circle, inviting the tweens to write one thing they admire or will remember about the person whose name is on the heart. Remind the tweens of Jesus' command to love one another.

When the hearts reach the person they belong to, have the tweens stand for the sending forth prayer.

Special Tips

The transition from the tweens fellowship into the youth fellowship can be a stressful time. Consider inviting your youth pastor or director, youth Sunday school teachers, and some youth fellowship leaders to attend the tweens' Ministry Fair to meet your "graduating" tweens.

Using older youth as helpers in the tweens fellowship throughout the year can also help make a smoother transition for tweens from one group to the other.

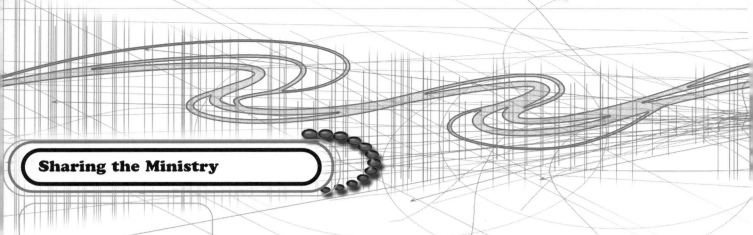

Notes

SENDING FORTH (2–5 minutes)

Say: **Today we reviewed our year together. We have shared fun times, sad times, joyful times, and some times that challenged our view of the world and ourselves.**

Before we close in prayer, you may share your concerns for yourself, your family, or others so that they may be lifted to God in prayer.

Allow each tween to write his or her concerns on paper so that they may be included in the closing prayer. Invite one of the tweens to lead the closing prayer printed below:

Pray: **Dear God, thank you for the time we have spent together. Help us send our graduating members off with joy. Help us welcome our newest members with hospitality. We pray for (*read the prayer concerns*). Thank you for hearing and responding to our prayers. In your name, we pray, Amen.**